Personalizing 21st Century Education

Personalizing 21ˢᵗ Century Education

A Framework for Student Success

Dan Domenech, Morton Sherman,
and John L. Brown

JOSSEY-BASS™
A Wiley Brand

Published by Jossey-Bass
A Wiley Brand
One Montgomery Street, Suite 1000, San Francisco, CA 94104–4594— www.josseybass.com

Jossey-Bass books and products are available through most bookstores. To contact Jossey-Bass directly call our Customer Care Department within the U.S. at 800-956-7739, outside the U.S. at 317-572-3986, or fax 317-572-4002.

Wiley publishes in a variety of print and electronic formats and by print-on-demand. Some material included with standard print versions of this book may not be included in e-books or in print-on-demand. If this book refers to media such as a CD or DVD that is not included in the version you purchased, you may download this material at http://booksupport.wiley.com. For more information about Wiley products, visit www.wiley.com.

Library of Congress Cataloging-in-Publication Data

ISBN 9781119080770 (Paperback)
ISBN 9781119080787 (ePDF)
ISBN 9781119080794 (ePub)

Cover image: Rob Lewine/Getty Images, Inc.
Cover design: Wiley

Printed in the United States of America

FIRST EDITION
PB Printing 10 9 8 7 6 5 4 3 2 1

It may seem odd that three individuals who have spent their careers as part of the "establishment" would offer as radical a departure from it as we present in the following pages. The fact is that educators have long wanted to be liberated from the regulatory chains that bind us and the twenty-first century has introduced the enabling technology to make personalized learning a reality. We dedicate this book to the future of public education in the United States and to those champions for children who will lead the transformation.

About the Authors

Daniel A. Domenech, PhD, is Executive Director AASA, the School Superintendents Association. Domenech has more than forty years of experience in public education, including twenty-seven years in the superintendency. For seven years Domenech served as superintendent of the Fairfax County, Virginia, Public Schools, the twelfth largest school system in the United States. He serves on numerous boards including the National and Virginia Boards for Communities in Schools.

Morton Sherman, EdD, is Associate Executive Director of AASA, the School Superintendents Association. Also with more than forty years of experience in public education, Sherman has served as a school superintendent in four states, including in Alexandria, Virginia, and Cherry Hill, New Jersey. He is the author of more than three hundred articles and has received national recognition for his work on mental health issues, community service, strategic planning, and the arts.

John L. Brown, PhD, is Executive Director of Curriculum Design and Instructional Services, Alexandria City Public Schools. He has also developed numerous professional publications for ASCD (including coauthoring *A Handbook for the Art and Science of Teaching* with Robert J. Marzano). He has also served as Director of Staff Development and Program Development for Prince George's County Public Schools, Maryland.

Contents

Preface: The Imperative for Transformation

Announcing the arrival of a new "Center for Personalized Health" in the greater Washington, D.C., area, a flier for INOVA Health touted the following innovations: "It will be a one-of-a-kind, internationally prominent center for genomic research, personalized health care, and associated life science commercial development," the notice explained, proudly declaring, "We've set our sights no lower than becoming the world's epicenter for translational cancer research and patient care." The notice then proceeded to sketch the various features of their "Personalized Medicine Education Center."

Although far from a new approach in the medical field, personalization has been steadily gaining traction in recent years. In the current medical model, a patient (at least one lucky enough to be well insured) generally enters a facility and receives personally tailored care, diagnosis, and treatment. Let's be clear from the beginning that personalization does not mean avoidance of goals and standards of practice. In fact, those standards are personally adjusted to meet individual needs. Such a personalized approach has become even more pronounced with the rise of "concierge" medicine, in which patients pay premiums for increased access, attention, and specialization.

This model (based on access, attention, and specialization, which are the hallmarks of personalization) can be found in many other areas. Several years ago a local chiropractor had his phone answered with a cheerful, "I can help you." How striking that is compared to "How can I help you?"

Department stores have personal shoppers. Hotels encourage and some chains expect that the staff provide caring, attentive, personalized service. Examples of personalized education are plentiful.

Yes, even in education we can find emerging examples of personalized efforts to help students learn well what we expect of them. These might be seen as personalized pathways, not races, to the dreams we hold for the children we serve. And they might be seen as counter to the lock step, this-is-the-way-it's-done approach that the recent Race to the Top encouraged.

We came to this project with one overarching question: *How can we raise the level of personalization in education so that each and every child learns to the highest, deepest, and broadest possible levels? What existing models might we look to for guidance, insight, and inspiration?* In education there is a long history of adhering to existing, traditional formulas and structures rather than adjusting to try to accommodate the needs of the student. This pattern needs to change. We need to find ways to modify or even radically rework this existing system to more adequately address the specific, varied needs of individual students. This health care flier was striking in that if we replaced the words *health* and *medicine* with *education* and *learning* we could already see the outlines for how to potentially restructure educational practices to incorporate the successful aspects of this more customer service–driven model.

Of course we recognize that for many, even mentioning the word *customer* when discussing education is close to sacrilege. In higher education, the growing trend toward treating students as customers has been a topic of distress and debate for quite some time. The line between business and education in higher education is indeed a very blurry distinction these days—a trend that, especially with the increasing number of charter schools, is quickly bleeding into secondary and elementary education as well.

We are not suggesting that we turn our schools into the Four Seasons hotels. Students are our center, our focus—they're not our customers. Such an analogy introduces the wrong mentality into the equation. But we *can* learn from customer service–based businesses and asset-driven models—models such as the development of personalization in medicine. We can draw on the positive aspects of these enterprises in our capitalistic society, taking and applying only their best aspects. We need to use all the tools that are available to us as we figure out how to create literate, participating, productive citizens in our society—and how to shape the future leaders, lawmakers, and teachers of our country.

We have strong feelings based on our personal and professional experiences that our schools must change. We know that the most significant change takes place at the classroom level, but without a change at the system level, individual classroom attempts will struggle, and perhaps fail, because of the system itself. Consider Horace Smith in Ted Sizer's classic *Horace's Compromise* (1984), who knew how to teach English but the responsibilities and expectations of the system diluted his efforts. We want to create systems in which the wonderful teachers, staff, and administrators who suffer as Horace Smith did can be given the opportunity to succeed with their students.

We certainly do not want to return to the days of shopping mall high schools. We believe in strong connections, clear expectations, and a highly trained diversified staff who can work with individuals and groups of students in very personalized environments.

The connections should be within the setting of a school and with the rest of the world. Technology makes this possible. Researchers, colleagues, entrepreneurs, parents, and members of the community are part of the learning and teaching teams.

We have been around long enough to remember when *Summerhill, Deschooling Society, Inequality, Why Johnny Can't Read, A Place Called School, Human Characteristics and School Learning,* and so many other classics of our profession were first published. What have we learned as a profession over the past fifty years since the Civil Rights Act was passed or the Elementary and Secondary Education Act was authorized? Let us take these challenges before us as a call unlike any we have heard before and create the educational systems that our children deserve. The imperative is clear because we see the purpose of public education is to help create literate, participating, productive citizens to sustain and even enhance our democracy.

Chapter 1

A Vision for Personalized Learning

- What does it mean for a student's education to be "personalized"?
- Why is personalization a potential solution to the problems of student disengagement and underachievement?
- What would a personalized learning environment look and feel like?

Personalized Learning—Articulating the Vision

Jillian is an eleven-year-old student who is still at home munching on her breakfast cereal while she looks at the screen of the notebook computer she received from her school. She is reviewing lessons that in the past would have been taught in school but now she does this work at home and discusses the implications with her classmates in school.

An hour later she arrives at school with other students and goes to a room where a group of them meet with Ms. Gabriel, their director of learning. Ms. Gabriel gives each student the activity schedule for the day. Jillian's first activity is a small-group discussion with four other students and an instructor in which they will analyze the assignment she was doing over breakfast.

Beatrice, Jillian's nine-year-old friend, is scheduled to attend a lecture on American history with a group of other students of various ages. Jonathan, who is the same age as Jillian, will stay with Ms. Gabriel for some tutoring in math.

Jillian's elementary school does not have grades. There are students there that range in age from five to twelve, but the students engage in independent work, small-group activities, one-on-one with a teacher, or in larger groups attending a lecture or watching a video. Age is never a factor in the groupings, only the readiness of the students for the level of instruction that they will be taught.

In each subject area the students advance as they reach the established level of mastery. Some students might accomplish mastery in a couple of days and others may require a week. Students progress at their own pace, with gentle prodding from the instructors when they sense that the students are not progressing as they should.

Assessment is ongoing, because most of the online programs used by the students monitor progress and automatically adjust the level of difficulty of the next lesson. In addition to formative assessment, the instructors use performance-based assessments to gauge progress. The director of learning responsible for a group of students is aware at all times of exactly where each student is relative to the standards that have been set in each subject area. This monitoring is also enabled by technology by using a program that keeps track of all the students the director of learning is responsible for.

The learners never miss out on their education. If Jillian is home sick, she can still access lessons online or carry on with her independent work or have an online session with an instructor. The same is true if schools are closed because of inclement weather. The traditional school calendar is a thing of the past. Schools are open year-round and students follow the schedule that has been set for them.

Jillian's friend Maria is a recent arrival from the Dominican Republic. She speaks very little English, but Maria's director of learning has assigned her activities and online programs that enable her to learn in her native Spanish while she is learning English. Maria is very good in math and she is able to participate in some math activities with the English-speaking students. Her lack of competence in English will not deter her from progressing in school and by the time she masters English she will quickly achieve mastery in other subject areas as well.

Remedial programs no longer exist because at all times each student is assigned activities that build on existing knowledge and skills. The same is true for students with special needs. Students move on to the middle school as they achieve mastery of the standards required for all elementary students. There is some accommodation for age so as not to have elementary students move on to the middle school at too young an age or have students staying at the elementary school too long. Decisions are made for each child based on maturation level in consultation with the parents. The same process applies to movement to the high school level.

The middle school and high school no longer group the students by periods. Both schools are also year-round and offer extended days. As is the case at the elementary level, students are assigned to a learning director who has the responsibility to develop an individualized learning plan for each student. The students are also involved in selecting and customizing their schedules, and they take required and elective courses in a number of ways, realizing full advantage of the available technology and the numerous ways the schools are organized for learning. Students also have the option of enrolling in college-level courses and getting college credits.

(continued)

(continued)

Because of the personal pacing, Jillian's bother, Chris, has met all of the requirements and will be graduating high school at age sixteen with a semester of college credits. Other students will require more time, but all who receive the diploma will have met the standards set for high school graduation.

BEGINNING THE JOURNEY: THE POWER OF PERSONALIZATION

We were at the Wright-Patterson Air Museum in Dayton, Ohio. Don Thompson was being installed as the incoming president for the American Association of School Administrators (AASA), and we were having a wonderful meal right under the huge wing of a space shuttle craft directly opposite one of the diminutive early crafts designed by the Wright brothers. Within a period of ninety years we had gone from being barely able to fly to flying to the outer reaches of earth's atmosphere and beyond.

Earlier that same day a group of us had visited an original one-room schoolhouse in Dayton, a model from the Wright brothers' time. Immediately apparent were the students' desks facing the front of the room toward the teacher's desk. Shelves along the sides of the room were filled with books while the walls held maps and pictures conducive to a proper learning environment. Put a couple of computers in that room and it would look like a 21st century classroom.

Although the advances in air travel over a 90-year period had been truly dramatic, a classroom today is not remarkably different from what it looked like at the beginning of the twentieth century. Indeed, our educational system today is still tied to an agrarian calendar, we still follow a grade-level structure that dates back to the beginning of the industrial revolution, and we still group students according to age, placing a number of them in a classroom with a teacher. Attempts to reform education simply try to make the existing structure more efficient rather than re-creating the basic concepts of teaching and learning.

We were recently at an event with Washington University professor Yong Zhao, who told us about one of Google's creations, the driverless car. Yong suggested that it was totally possible that within a short period of time, the driverless car would be a part of our lives and challenged us to imagine what life would be like. We took to the task and set about creating a vision of a world in which people would no longer drive. Driving schools would go out of business; so would motor vehicle bureaus, at least the driving license–issuing department; police would no longer issue tickets for speeding or driving under the influence of alcohol. The changes to the world as we know it would be dramatic, all because cars would drive themselves—changes similar to how the airplane has changed our lives over the last century.

DRIVERLESS CARS AND THE FUTURE OF 21ST CENTURY EDUCATION

What if we applied Zhao's driverless car exercise to education? What if we were asked to imagine a world in which the educational system revolved around teaching a single student? Forget about the educational system as we know it today. Reconstruct a system that focuses on teaching one student at a time. Can we do it and how would we do it? This essential question raises many others:

- How much of what is part of the system today would remain?
- Would the new system be able to achieve the goal of closing the achievement gap?
- Would it resolve the economic gap created by how we fund education?
- Would there be a need for remediation services, summer school, after-school programs, and the practice of not promoting children to the next grade? Would we need classrooms or school buildings for that matter?
- Would all students be expected to graduate after thirteen years of schooling?
- Would we need to assess all students at the same time with the same tests?
- Would we need report cards and grades?

We could let our imagination run wild with all the possibilities, because we would focus on educating a single student as opposed to group after group after group of pupils.

WHAT IS A PERSONALIZED 21ST CENTURY EDUCATION?

What is personalized learning? There is no agreement on one definition. In most cases today personalized learning refers to some form of blended learning in which software programs are used that adapt to the ability level of a child. It may also be used to define programs in which the teacher employs differentiated instruction. These are approximations of what personalized learning could be at the classroom level, but they do not encompass the systemic transformation that we envision.

In our version of personalized learning we envision a transformation in how children are taught and how the system organizes for learning. Each child is treated as a unique individual and his or her education begins with the development of a personalized education plan. The child is assessed in each of the subjects to be taught and, based on the assessments, integrated lesson plans are developed that builds on what the child already knows, with instructional strategies designed for his or her ability level. Material that is beyond the child's ability level will not be introduced. Consequently, the child will not experience the frustration of sitting for a lesson that is too difficult to grasp and learn. Similarly, the student will not be exposed to material that has already been assimilated, avoiding the boredom and wasted time that occurs when a child is being taught a lesson already learned. Instruction will always build on the child's existing knowledge and capabilities, thus fostering continual progress.

The child is part of a group of students assigned to the teacher, who is responsible for devising a personalized education plan for each learner. That plan will include activities when the teacher will work with the student one-on-one. There will also be activities when the teacher will work with a small group of students who are at the same stage in terms of the material to be learned and are at the same ability level.

Instances will occur in which a large group of the students will be exposed to a lesson, video, guest lecture appropriate to the ability levels and the base knowledge of the entire group. Taking advantage of the existing technology, students will also make use of the appropriate devices and programs to take independent online lessons and online sessions with teachers. Those sessions could take place in the school, at home, or anywhere where the student has a computer and access to the lesson. Sickness and snow days will no longer prevent the child from engaging in the learning process.

In a personalized learning environment students will not have to be grouped in a grade according to their age. Grouping will be done according to proficiency level rather than age. Current practice indicates that the grouping should not span more than three years, particularly in the early elementary grades when maturation is a factor. In this environment students will never be rated below or above grade level because there will be no grades. The student's progress will be measured against the standards that all students will be required to meet. Formative assessments to monitor student progress against those standards will be necessary to ensure continual progress.

Because not all children learn at the same rate, personalized learning will enable students to learn at their own pace. Some children will advance very quickly and others will require more time. By current standards, we could see students graduating high school at ages that could span from fifteen to twenty-one. It would depend on the acceptance of a set of standards that would require students to have mastered the minimum requirements in order to receive a high school diploma, in essence turning the document into a competency-based certificate rather than a completion diploma based on thirteen years of schooling.

The role of the teacher changes dramatically in a personalized learning environment. Rather than the sage on the stage, the teacher becomes a director of learning. Teachers are trained to assess, diagnose, and develop a personalized learning plan for each student. They become experts in prescribing the appropriate strategy that will maximize their students' ability to learn. Rather than developing a lesson plan for an entire class, they must develop a lesson plan for each child along with selecting the appropriate materials, groups, and venue in which the instruction will take place. This will need to be a team effort in which a differentiated staffing approach will be helpful.

In the mid-1960s the Kettering Foundation in Dayton, Ohio, developed a program called *Individually Guided Education* that created a framework that was intended to facilitate instruction in a multiaged, nongraded, continual progress environment. Unfortunately, back in 1965 we did not have the technological advances that we have today to support such a system.

In a personalized learning environment the child progresses at her or his own pace. The learner with special needs and achievement issues is not left behind and the gifted child can progress without being held back. At this stage we can begin to envision the multitude of barriers that would stand in the way of making personalized learning a reality. After so many years, can we dispense with grade levels and grouping kids by age? Are we ready to accept that if we truly want all children to learn, we will have to enable them to progress at their own pace. Can we do away with the "edifice complex" and accept that children can learn in environments other than the school building. Are we ready to erase the slate and start from scratch in truly transforming education from what is to what it can be if the system is redesigned to educate one child at a time?

HOW DID WE GET HERE? HOW CAN WE GET OUT?

The current education system is convenient for the adults, not necessarily for the children whom it is intended to serve. The current age-determined grade-level structure mimicked the industrial revolution's assembly line. In spite of the fact that child psychology has for years told us that children develop at different rates, we continue to conveniently group children of the same age in the same grade level. Kindergarten is for five-year-olds and students are supposed to finish high school around the time they turn eighteen.

Because it is not practical to have a teacher for every child, we assign groups of students to a teacher who then proceeds to teach them as a group, in spite of the range of aptitudes that will exist within the group. The typical approach is to teach to the middle of the group, beginning a process in which the more capable students get bored with what is going on and the less capable students are lost and become candidates for remediation, summer school, getting left back, and eventually dropping out of school.

The school calendar itself is a throwback to the nineteenth century. Schools are typically closed during the summer months because back in the day the children were needed to help with harvesting of the crops. Again, in spite of the fact that we know how detrimental to learning two months away from school can be, we retain the calendar because it is convenient for the adults. It is also convenient for the resort and entertainment industry. When Dan Domenech was a Virginia superintendent, for years he attempted to get rid of what is known in Virginia as the King's Dominion Bill, a piece of legislation that requires schools to start after Labor Day so that students and their families will not miss out on the opportunity to spend that last wonderful weekend of summer at an amusement park such as the bill's namesake.

Schools tend to be locked into a set number of school days per year and a set number of hours per day, again because it is convenient for the adults. Such is the case when we need to organize for the teaching of groups of students. Depending on the school district's financial resources, students will be assigned to classes of anywhere from fifteen to forty students, or more. We have also divided knowledge into distinct subject areas so that we teach language arts, math, science, history, music, art, physical education, and so on as separate courses. At the elementary level this can lead to teaching subject areas in which the instructor may be lacking expertise.

The school curriculum takes each subject area and spirals it in terms of levels of difficulty so that students are often learning the same things but at higher levels of difficulty as they grow older and move up the grades. Because teachers have to deal with a group of students at the same time, they seldom have the opportunity to work with a struggling student one-on-one. Students begin to fall further and further behind and at the end of the school year, if they are promoted, they move on to the next grade level where the very subject that they could not understand is now being taught at a higher degree of difficulty. But perhaps they will not be promoted and will have to repeat the same grade and be exposed again to all of the things they did not learn as well as the many they did learn, out of convenience for the adults.

A VISION FOR PERSONALIZED EDUCATION IN THE 21ST CENTURY

The typical solutions for helping students catch up generally do not work. Children pulled out of their classrooms to receive remediation services tend to miss what is going on in their classroom while they are out and fall further behind. Those who attend summer school because they did not succeed after ten months of instruction are expected to master the subject in four to five weeks. Curriculum and pacing guides require that students keep up with the instruction because there is a specified amount of material that they have to learn, regardless of the student's ability to keep up with the pace. There can be no slowing down for a single child because so many chapters have to be "covered" prior to the end of the school year.

In recent years the standard assessment and accountability movements have exacerbated the problem for many students. Students are expected to have acquired a certain amount of knowledge by a certain age, and they will be tested to see if that is so, totally ignoring the fact that we know that children learn at different paces. Consequently, the opportunity to teach a child at a pace appropriate to his or her ability is discounted because all children are expected to know this by a certain grade level. Throw into the mix the ongoing reality that we now hold teachers accountable for whether the students in the class have all learned what they are expected to learn by the end of that grade level.

We submit to you that all of the problems we have stipulated in this chapter will disappear if we convert the current education system to one that focuses on personalized learning. Let us begin with a blank slate and build from there. The tools are available right now. Our technological advances make it totally possible. We have to rebuild and reorganize but we do not have to throw out the baby with the bath water. The good news is that many districts are already doing bits and pieces of what a personalized educational system should look like.

There are major implications for our legislators and policy makers. We have too many laws, rules, and regulations that are an impediment to personalized learning. We will need to get rid of those. There is a considerable amount of required retraining for our educational professionals. As we have suggested previously, teachers will need to become directors of learning rather than sages on the stage. Administrators will need to learn to coordinate the many resources and venues that will be necessary to truly personalize learning.

Parents will have to get used to a new school culture in which their child will not be in a grade; they may, when appropriate, be grouped with children older or younger; and, rather than getting a grade for the student, they will be told the skills and level of performance their child has mastered relative to the uniform set of standards all children are expected to attain but without a specific time limit.

Seat-time requirements will be passé, because students will be able to learn anywhere without always having to be in the classroom, thus ridding ourselves of the edifice complex. Students will interact with many instructors who will fulfill the individualized education program developed for the child by the lead teacher. Because each child will be progressing at all times at the pace appropriate for his or her ability, there will not be a need for remediation. Some children will actually be able to graduate high school at a much younger age if they have fulfilled the standards prescribed by their district and state, and perhaps the nation. Other students may need to be in schools beyond eighteen years of age in order to fulfill the aforementioned standards. Similar to the world with driverless cars, it will be a very different place when each child receives a personalized education.

QUESTIONS FOR REFLECTION AND DISCUSSION BY STRATEGIC PLANNING TEAMS

1. What is our vision for a personalized education?

2. To what extent do we agree—or disagree—with the claims and assertions made in this chapter?

3. How practical or feasible would it be for schools and districts to "begin with a blank slate and build from there"?

4. To what extent does our school or district reflect the characteristics of the old industrial model presented here?

5. What aspects of our school or district reflect features of a commitment to personalizing learning?

Chapter 2

Personalizing the System, Not Just the Classroom

There is a relentless attack on our public education system that would have the U.S. public believe that we have some of the worst schools in the world. Yet, if we were to gauge our educational system by the very measures that are used to hold us accountable, it turns out that the United States' public schools today are performing as well as they ever have.

According to the National Assessment for Educational Progress (NAEP), otherwise known as the Nation's Report Card, our third- and eighth-grade scores in reading and math are the highest that they have ever been. The nation's drop-out rate is the lowest ever, and high school graduation rates are at an all-time high. College attendance rates are high and African American and Latino students are performing better than ever. Similarly, the Gallup Poll suggests that parents with children in school give their public schools the highest approval rating ever, and the general public's attitude toward our schools—although lower than what parents give—has remained static over a 20-year period.

So why do we hear so many complaints and grievances about public education? There appears to be a growing recognition that our current model of schooling is outworn and insufficient to address the demands of a change-driven, technology-focused world. Too many children of color and socioeconomic disadvantage are failing. In most cases, many of these students also happen to be the children who live in poverty. Our student population is now minority majority. The current system is failing poor minority students.

The National Assessment of Educational Progress (NAEP) – often referred to as the Nation's Report Card – confirms that student performance on this assessment correlates almost perfectly with learner's socioeconomic status. A graph charting NAEP performance against the percentage of students on free and reduced lunches shows almost a perfect negative correlation. NAEP performance is highest in schools with low percentages of children on free and reduced lunches. Conversely, NAEP performance is the lowest in schools with the highest concentrations of children on free and reduced lunches.

Doing away with poverty might be seen as the obvious solution to this dilemma, but our country has had an ongoing political, economic, and cultural war on poverty throughout much of its history. Our poverty rates are on the rise, not on the decline. Many attempts have been made to reform our public school system, but we have failed to close the pernicious achievement gap between the haves and the have-nots. According to many—including the popular media—the rich appear to be getting significantly richer and the poor are getting increasingly poorer. Those who argue that money makes no difference should consider why the rich send their children to the best and most expensive private schools instead of public schools. In our nation's capital you can count on one hand the number of lawmakers who send their children to the DC public schools.

Paul Batalden, the well-known organizational improvement scientist, once said that every system is perfectly designed to achieve the results it gets. Our public school system was designed to get the results we are getting. It is meant to sort our students, not ensure that they all perform at a proficiency level that will fully prepare them for success in the 21st Century. We will never achieve our goal of eliminating the achievement gap and "leaving no child behind" unless we change the system itself. Current efforts at reform through charter schools, vouchers, choice, teacher evaluation, and high-handed accountability are merely trying to improve the current system, not change it.

Two of this book's authors are boaters who are fastidious about maintaining their boats in tip-top shape. Regardless of the condition of the boat, however, it will never go faster than its design will allow it to go. We are trying to make our school system go faster than it was designed to go. Structurally, it is going as fast as it can, given the priorities it is asked to address. But we will never achieve the equity we seek among all of our students until we change the system itself.

We assert that personalized education is the solution. However, personalizing education for the individual learner must occur within a system that values and promotes personalization at the individual, classroom, school, and macro levels. When all parts of a system are focused on the individual student—rather than groups of learners—we can provide all students with the exact instruction they require at a particular point in time and over the course of their personal development. In such a system, many things are possible. For example:

- Non-English-speaking students can be taught English without holding back the English-speaking students in the class. If there are available instructors who speak the child's language, they can be called on to spend part of the time instructing the child in his or her native language. There are available software and online programs that can be used to instruct the child in the native language and English at home or in school.

- A child is never remediated because instruction is always at the appropriate level of difficulty and proficiency for the child in every content area.

- Time is not a factor because instruction proceeds at the appropriate pace for the child.

- Diversity and poverty are not an issue when each child gets the education that has been designed to meet her or his needs. The end result will be parity because not only will every student finish the race but also the race itself will be designed to ensure outcomes necessary for success in our world today—not the assembly-line world that modern education was first designed to address.

TEN BUILDING BLOCKS OF A SUCCESSFUL PERSONALIZED 21ST CENTURY EDUCATIONAL SYSTEM

In this next section, we establish the framework that will guide and inform this entire book. We have identified ten major system-level factors that are the non-negotiable building blocks of an effective and personalized 21st century educational system:

1. **Creating a vision for 21st century education.** Building consensus about the significance of personalization as a non-negotiable priority in schools and systems reflective of true 21st century learning

2. **Dealing with diversity.** Transforming current organizational design and practice to accommodate the growing diversity of student populations in schools today

3. **Identifying benchmarks and exemplars of schools and districts already personalizing students' education.** Discovering schools that succeed in personalizing the learning environment, addressing every learner's intellectual, social-emotional, relational, and physical developmental needs

4. **Transforming curriculum and programs of study.** Providing an aspirational curriculum for every learner, ensuring that blended learning and access to learning is a twenty-four-hour pathway for all students

5. **Personalizing teaching and learning.** Transforming the impact of education through a greater focus on the needs and strengths of the individual learner, providing students with many more options about where and how they learn (including growing focus on independent inquiry, project-based learning, and truly differentiated learning tasks)

6. **Transforming systems of accountability—making assessment meaningful.** Moving away from the current standardized testing fixation approach in favor of authentic, learner-focused, and performance-based assessment tasks and projects

7. **Maximizing the impact of technology and support resources.** Ensuring that we find answers to the challenge of the digital divide and use technology and other support resources in an organic, holistic way—rather than our current emphasis on remediation

8. **Personalizing leadership and governance.** Exploring and implementing new approaches to decision making and problem solving, including use of economic resources; distributing leadership and governance responsibilities to empower individuals and groups at the most immediate levels of participation; revolutionizing traditional notions of administration, supervision, and human resource management

9. **Personalizing health, social, and psychological services.** Providing a true pre-K–graduation support system that successfully addresses all students' social and psychological development, including immediate access to health and wellness services and resources and maximizing family access to a range of support services

10. **Capitalizing on the power of parent, community, and cross-institutional partnerships.** Inviting key stakeholder groups into the process of personal-

izing education, expanding student access to a range of mentors, coaches, and educational pathways; making cross-institutional partnerships a direct means for supporting personalization

BUILDING BLOCK 1: CREATING A VISION FOR 21ST CENTURY EDUCATION

The first and primary building block for personalizing a school district is to build consensus about what—exactly—personalization means. We argue that this vision should encompass the entire school system—not just individual classrooms. At the heart of this personalization process is the need to view all parts of a system as interdependent and governed by common values, norms, standards, and practices. If a specific district retains an industrial paradigm—a collective mind-set that reinforces the need for standardization, discrete and test-driven accountability, and a top-down approach to governance and management—the starting point in this journey is to build consensus about the necessity of a paradigmatic counterpoint.

Our vision is that entire school systems move toward decentralization and personalization. Curriculum becomes aspirational and reflective of true twenty-first-century workplace competencies—including collaborative problem solving, decision making, and long-range strategic planning. The whole learner—including the academic-intellectual, social-emotional, and physical aspects of being human—are a recurrent emphasis and focal point. Data gathering about students' discrete acquisition of facts and skills in isolation diminishes (or disappears altogether), replaced by an emphasis on authentic, problem- and project-based assessment with the learner at the heart of his or her own learning process.

Similarly, the term *learner* expands to include virtually every human being within a personalized educational system. Every adult is a lifelong learner, too. Professional development, governance, and management become catalysts for learning, rather than strongholds of accountability and standardization. Social, psychological, and health services are a fundamental part of the well-being of every systemic learner.

Perhaps most significantly, a personalized system expands the notion of a learning environment to include the entire planet, not just the confines of a single classroom. Technology—particularly information accessing and online investigation—becomes a true norm for all learners. The planet as school workplace becomes an essential part of this vision.

Vision Move beyond the industrial model of education that still guides and informs many public schools and school systems today. Transform education to reflect the realities of the twenty-first century, including the need for personalization, differentiation, authenticity, rigor, and engagement.

Current Reality Education remains fixed within individual school sites. Resources and logistics frequently limit educators' ability to make the world the stage on which students' education functions.

Implementation Steps
1. Explore models and exemplar sites that reflect aspects of a personalized approach to education.
2. Create a systemic vision and mission statement along with a set of guiding principles to shape and inform the transformation process.
3. Explore that following axiom: All the world's a classroom; the lesson dictates the venue.
4. Reconsider the need for discrete buildings and discrete classrooms.
5. Maximize the opportunities offered by the electronic world in which we live.
6. Create personalized schedules rather than seat time or Carnegie Units.

Pushback and Predictable Resistance As suggested in many of the other building blocks, traditional notions of schools as buildings with discrete classrooms remain the norm. Inevitable resistance will include skepticism about the possibilities of achieving this vision and fears about its implications for non-standardized accountability.

BUILDING BLOCK 2: DEALING WITH DIVERSITY

In recent years the United States has earned the unfortunate distinction of having the highest childhood poverty rate among industrialized nations. One out of every four children lives in poverty. In addition, the economic recession we have endured since 2008 has resulted in one out of twenty children being homeless. These are statistics that hardly befit the richest and most powerful nation in the world.

Additionally, we are entering an era in which countries such as the United States are becoming increasingly diverse, with Black and Hispanic students outnumbering white students. Challenges resulting from this demographic change must be addressed in a personalized school system—just as the growing numbers of English language learners in our school populations require specialized, and truly personalized, approaches to their education.

Vision Personalize how the individual student is educated, including aligning curriculum content with student readiness levels, interests, and learner profiles. We must also place more expansive focus on progress monitoring and on-the-spot formative assessment and coaching-driven feedback to every learner. Expand the notion of education as a lifelong journey not confined to a single building. Capitalize on the power of the environment and region in which students live as the ultimate schoolhouse.

Current Reality Many school systems are struggling with growing numbers of free- and reduced-lunch populations as well as the cultural complexity, challenges, and opportunities that come with demographic diversity. Standardized industrial models of education—with their focus on test-generated achievement results—are no longer viable in a pluralistic and diverse twenty-first-century world.

Implementation Steps Use demographic data (particularly disaggregated data patterns for groups and individual students) to address key organizational transformation priorities:

1. Push all students to achieve at the highest level.

2. Redefine what we mean by the term *achievement gap*.

3. Prioritize equity, not equality—getting all students to achieve "greater knots" (to use an old boating metaphor).

4. Move away from business models of data management in favor of individualized student progress monitoring.

5. Ensure that all students achieve the meta-skills required for success in a changed-dominated, technology-driven 21st century global economy.

Pushback and Predictable Resistance Systems have standardized practices and assessment processes firmly integrated into their organizational structures and cultures. The lure of returning to the basics and data-based high-stakes accountability measures is a rearview mirror, causing many educators and politicians to resist change. The need for personalization—especially for diverse student populations—is an essential part of genuine and effective differentiation, but many systems and schools are currently organized to work counter to this practice.

BUILDING BLOCK 3: IDENTIFYING BENCHMARKS AND EXEMPLARS OF SCHOOLS AND DISTRICTS ALREADY PERSONALIZING STUDENTS' EDUCATION

Once the stakeholders in a school system have generated a consensus-driven vision for personalization and a commitment to addressing the emerging diversity issues of their district, it is useful for strategic planning groups to consider what is working in personalized school settings today. This process can begin by investigating the schools and organizations identified throughout this book, including site visits and tours of each school's website.

However, strategic planning teams must also begin to consider how these exemplary sites manage to swim against the tides of standardization and test-driven accountability. For example, how does each school coexist with others in more traditional school system settings? What were the strategies, processes, and resources they required to make the leap into the twenty-first century?

Inevitably, educators and community members will ask these questions. In particular, they will need to explore ways to overcome anxiety about test-driven performance targets and emerging systems of teacher evaluation predicated on such targets. What does accountability look like in new, personalized educational settings? What benchmarks will the strategic planning team need to propose and advocate for as their system moves toward personalization?

Vision Develop a toolkit or compilation of school and district profiles of exemplar sites already effective in demonstrating one or more best practices related to personalization.

Current Reality A majority of school models offer traditional curriculum based in discrete standards and organized around discrete content areas and grade levels. Minimal opportunities exist for true personalized learning. Even the term *differentiation* is frequently used so loosely that clear operational definitions and signpost indicators are absent.

Implementation Steps In acquiring a compendium of models and exemplar sites, strategic planning team members may wish to consider how such sites address the following issues:

1. Building stakeholder consensus about the meaning of personalization and its importance as a controlling value within the school or district

2. Discovering how the personalized education offered by the school or district addresses the needs of socioeconomically, linguistically, and ethnically diverse students, including those with interrupted formal education

3. Analyzing the design and implementation of an aspirational curriculum accessible to all students

4. Ensuring that the teaching-learning process reflects best practices in personalization and differentiation

5. Investigating the assessment and evaluation systems underlying accountability within the school or district: *To what extent are they balanced and genuinely personalized?*

6. Exploring the governance and management structures and processes underlying system operations

7. Determining if the whole learner truly is at the center of academic, social, psychological, and health services—including the adult learner within the system

8. Examining the extent to which stakeholder individuals and groups are an active and positive part of personalization within the school or district

Pushback and Predictable Resistance It goes without saying that when educators and community members explore the concept of personalization, there will be skepticism about such issues as the progressive, some would say romanticized, notion of true personalization. Stakeholders must find ways to internalize the inherent possibilities of personalized education, including its clear and transparent connection to the technology-driven and collaborative nature of many 21st century workplaces today.

BUILDING BLOCK 4: TRANSFORMING CURRICULUM AND PROGRAMS OF STUDY

There is no more politically volatile arena in education these days than the issue of what students should learn, when they should learn it, and how they can best learn what is required. Aspirational curriculum suggests that the individual learner is the heart of the curriculum, not just state or locally mandated standards that may be assessed on a standardized test.

We view curriculum as a system that involves students' total educational experience. All parts of the curriculum must support one another to help the individual learner become as successful and engaged as possible. Reductionist approaches to preparing students for standardized tests must be replaced by a comprehensive, integrated, and holistic approach to each whole child as he or she progresses through the experience of public or private education.

Vision View curriculum as a multifaceted system for promoting the individual growth and success of every learner, ensuring that every student is engaged in education as a lifelong pursuit. Every student should become a critical thinker and creator, exploring interests and avenues of personal aspiration and engagement.

Current Reality Standardization is frequently the norm, with a growing national obsession with "unpacking" standards in isolation. The assessed or tested curriculum drives and fuels teaching and learning in many districts, especially urban centers.

Implementation Steps Create curricula that place the learner at the center of the learning process, including the following key steps:

1. Articulate a vision and mission that emphasizes personalization and the whole learner—not simply individual performance on state or local tests.

2. Ensure that curriculum alignment is a priority, with the guiding principles of personalization actively integrated into the following:

    The Ideal Curriculum The aspirations and guiding principles of personalization are clearly articulated in mission and vision statements and related public documents.

    The Written Curriculum Written curriculum guides and related support documents (e.g., lesson plans) reinforce the spirit and intent of personalization, addressing students' varying readiness levels, interests, and learner profiles.

The Assessed Curriculum The personalized school and district diminish the focus on standardized testing and replace it with a more balanced approach to student progress monitoring, including sustained use of diagnostic and formative assessment and coaching-based feedback as well as student portfolios and work collections.

The Supported Curriculum Textbooks, support materials, and electronic resources expand students' options for personal investigation based on interests and areas of need.

The Taught Curriculum The classroom becomes a truly personalized environment in which the learner is the center of the experience, not just the prescribed content. The instructor becomes a true coach and facilitator, encouraging individual expression, investigation, and learning pathways.

The Learned Curriculum All students demonstrate proficiency in mastering identified standards, but they have multiple opportunities and experiences to display their knowledge, skills, and understanding in a variety of formats, domains, and performance tasks.

The Elimination of a Hidden Curriculum Students and staff arrive at a point where there is no inherent contradiction between what the vision and mission suggest about personalized learning and the ways in which learning is monitored and evaluated.

Pushback and Predictable Resistance The process of personalization requires a true paradigm shift in learning organizations. There will be inevitable pushback related to issues of standardized testing, including political pressures related to accountability and data analysis.

BUILDING BLOCK 5: PERSONALIZED TEACHING AND LEARNING

A major component of building an educational culture of personalization involves the use of time. Our current models of class periods emphasize discrete time measures to delineate when subjects such as English begin and mathematics and science end. Personalized learning will require a very different approach to scheduling and time allocation. More on-the-spot decision making must occur, involving choices between the instructor and the student.

With the elimination of time as a factor (as is currently the case when we expect all children of the same age to accomplish the same things at the same time), children would then have the opportunity to take the time they need to grasp more complex cognitive factors. Instructors will not feel pressured to run through lesson after lesson in order to complete the syllabus prior to the end of the school year. A current third-grader doing first-grade work will not feel "dumb" or "slow" because he or she cannot do the same work as other kids in the class. Conversely our more capable students will not feel held back because the teacher is pacing instruction to the middle of the pack.

The elimination of time as a factor will also enable teachers to delve deeper into helping students to become creative thinkers and problem solvers, encouraging students to explore all elements of a concept rather than just the shallow basics because we are in a rush to move on. The fundamental nature of our spiraling curriculum is that we teach the same thing at every grade level but each time at just a slightly higher level of difficulty.

Teaching one child at a time is very different than teaching a group of students. We cannot imagine a single teacher that would not want the opportunity to be free of the pressure of having to teach a group of students simultaneously and be expected to achieve the same results with all of the students within the same time frame.

Working in teams with other teachers will enable instructors to work one-on-one with students or with small groups or lecture large groups or monitor the performance of students working on their own, either online or on individual projects. Rather than being isolated in a classroom, teachers will be trained to collaborate and work as a team or professional learning community.

> **Vision** Personalized learning will require a major shift in culture. We will need to abandon current organizational and scheduling practice in common use today in favor of personalized scheduling. We must make the move toward schools without traditional grades and without standardized time requirements and allocations.

> **Current Reality** Once again, standardization is the norm rather than the exception. Current school reform models typically derive from business

models rather than personalized approaches to the teaching-learning process.

Implementation Steps   Begin to explore alternatives to traditional teaching-learning models. Consider scenarios such as the following:

1.   A group of 25 students might be assigned to a teacher.

2.   The group might be fairly homogeneous in terms of ability and competency but not age.

3.   The teacher would be responsible for developing a personalized learning plan for each student for a cycle of time and would prescribe groupings (individual, small, large) appropriate for the activity to be engaged in.

4.   The technology used by the student will have embedded assessments that will enable the teacher to monitor the student's performance for each assigned task.

5.   Corrections will be made to the learning plan as appropriate.

Pushback and Predictable Resistance   The approaches described here go against traditional ideas of the teacher as the center of the classroom. There will be inevitable resistance related to concerns such as student self-management, discipline, test preparation, and the complexity of the new model. A major commitment to professional development—reinforced through lesson study and peer modeling—will be necessary for this vision to become a reality in most schools and systems.

BUILDING BLOCK 6: TRANSFORMING SYSTEMS OF ACCOUNTABILITY—MAKING ASSESSMENT MEANINGFUL

A true personalized learning environment will remain relatively free of typical test-driven accountability restraints. Ideally, a personalized learning system enables a balanced approach to assessment and evaluation, one that integrates diagnostic assessment, formative assessment, and summative assessment. Increasingly, we will see less and less evidence of overreliance on standardized testing as a measure of success.

Instead, we will see students assuming increasing responsibility for their own learning—and determining in partnership with their teachers the multiple ways in which they can demonstrate their achievement and learning progress. Student portfolio assessment will become the norm, including electronic artifacts of student work products and performances. Additionally, such portfolio assessments will require that students reflect on, critique, and improve their work products to show increasing levels of proficiency, competence, and independent transfer.

School systems will need to revise and reform their approach to record keeping as well as student-progress monitoring. Traditional grading systems as we now know them will decline in importance and use, replaced by electronic data systems capable of truly reflecting student progress in relationship to multiple standards and performance domains.

This approach will also require cross-institutional partnerships in which organizations such as colleges, universities, and corporations learn to use new data sources to understand individual student profiles, strengths, and areas in need of improvement. In effect, a continuum of learning growth (in hard and soft skills such as collaboration, time management, self-regulation, and problem solving) will underlie 21st century personalized systems of accountability and progress monitoring.

> **Vision** Move away from a fixation on standardized testing and test-driven accountability in favor of multiple approaches to monitoring students' mastery of standards. Reinforce the authentic curriculum with a range of real assessments, including electronic portfolios and other real-world measures.

> **Current Reality** Increasingly, we see a focus on tests driving the accountability systems in multiple regions and areas, including teacher evaluations predicated on standardized data results.

> **Implementation Steps**
> 1. Make transparent what every student should know, do, and understand.
> 2. Monitor progress in the individual, not by grade level or age groups.
> 3. Focus accountability on meeting the individual student's needs in a personalized and engaging way rather than the objectification and standardization of modern testing.

> **Pushback and Predictable Resistance** The current focus on standardization and statistical analysis reinforces a commitment to a limited portrait of student achievement. Educators, parents, and the broader community will

need to become comfortable with alternative measures of student progress. These efforts are still entrapped in the traditional grade-level structure and horde mentality.

BUILDING BLOCK 7: MAXIMIZING THE IMPACT OF TECHNOLOGY AND SUPPORT RESOURCES

It goes without saying that technology has transformed the 21st century workplace and global environment. We are instantly connected and interconnected, yet the true power of technology in education is not keeping pace with the changes it is bringing to the modern world of work. Personalized schools and systems will need to ensure that technology is an organic and constantly upgrading component of the personalization process.

Technology plays a major role in enabling personalized learning. The notion of individualizing instruction has been around for years, but we have never had the resources to make it work. It was too labor intensive and required an inordinate amount of teacher preparation. With the advent of digitized materials, access to the world via the Internet, and online courses and assessments, teachers can organize for personalized learning as they never could before.

> **Vision** Incorporate the leap to digital learning into the educational environment. Use this leap to encourage a movement toward personalized learning such as blended learning and virtual schools.

> **Current Reality** Although schools are making strides toward incorporating technology into students' everyday experience, true and organic integration is lacking.

> **Implementation Steps** Help every learner have a true 21st century education through these ways:

> 1. Blended learning

> 2. Flipped classrooms

> 3. Technology as an organic part of student learning (beyond the computer tutorial model)

> 4. Online learning

Pushback and Predictable Resistance Although many advocate for the use of technology, budget cuts and fiscal limitations prevent the full realization of this part of the vision for personalizing education. Comprehensive professional development is also necessary to overcome limited notions of technology integration.

BUILDING BLOCK 8: PERSONALIZING LEADERSHIP AND GOVERNANCE

Adjustments will also have to be made in how we staff our schools. A differentiated staffing arrangement would best serve personalized learning from economic and academic perspectives. A team made up of a master teacher, several teachers, instructional aids, along with a technology specialist could effectively work with several hundred students and maintain an affordable student-instructor ratio.

In a personalized education system we will know how students are progressing in real time. Federal or state agencies might want to know how many students have reached a specified level of proficiency at a given date and how many students fail to exit the system (graduate) by their twenty-first birthday. They could also record the number of students that exit the system at different ages, although that would most likely be because of economics and demographics, as is the case today.

Vision Administrators will assist the teachers in the coordination of the various groupings and provide the curriculum and instructional resources needed to address the needs of each child, with the appropriate technology being a major factor.

Current Reality Our current system of accountability requires schools to make adequate yearly progress, which is based on a percentage of students reaching a specified level of proficiency on the standardized tests administered by the state. The tests are administered to all students at specified grade levels.

Implementation Steps
1. Coordinate human and materials resources to reinforce appropriate and equitable access for all learners.

2. Encourage teaching as a facilitative model in which instructors are coaches and facilitators of learning, rather than dispensers of information.

3. Introduce the concept of educators as change agents, rather than supporters of the status quo.

4. View instructional leaders and administrators as culture builders committed to promoting an organization that is collaborative and cross-functional.

5. Differentiate staffing to ensure maximum student access to experts in the teaching-learning-assessment process.

6. Reinforce that parents are the first true teacher, ensuring that they are encouraged to play an active and supportive role in their child's education.

7. Expand the organization and structure inherent in the teaching profession, including options for career ladders that include master teachers, well-trained support personnel, apprenticeships, and mentors.

8. Increase the power and range of cross-institutional partnerships, including parents and community partners.

Pushback and Predictable Resistance Those of us who have attempted to personalize learning in our systems are familiar with pushback from parents. Introducing a system that is radically different from what parents experienced when they went to school will require a great deal of parent and community education. Parents will insist on knowing what grade their child is in and what letter or number grades they are getting in their subjects of study. Never mind that the students are progressing at their own pace and achieving mastery of the skills and standards prescribed prior to moving to the next set of standards.

BUILDING BLOCK 9: PERSONALIZING HEALTH, SOCIAL, AND PSYCHOLOGICAL SERVICES

The entrenched traditions of standardization and data-based accountability are frequently accompanied by a lack of focus on aspects of students' development other than the cognitive academic. In a genuinely personalized twenty-first-century educational system, the whole child—and all his or her needs, strengths, and potentials—becomes a priority.

Progress monitoring and assessment-evaluation systems in transformed educational systems must take into account students' varying developmental, psychological, social-emotional, and physical needs. Given the growing levels of diversity—including racial, ethnic, linguistic, and socioeconomic—in schools and districts today, it is essential that the total child be monitored, not just his or her ability to retrieve declarative knowledge on a standardized test.

Vision Create school systems that value and successfully address all aspects of human growth and development, including students' physical needs, social-emotional progress, capacity for relationship building, and physical growth and needs. A personalized system not only prioritizes all aspects of child growth and development but also reinforces them throughout the teaching-learning process.

Current Reality Although counselors, psychologists, and social workers are traditionally part of most school system's human resources pool, many schools today do not address with any depth child development beyond the cognitive academic. There is also evidence that the unique developmental issues and needs associated with children's various age levels (e.g., the challenges of early learning years, the tumult of early adolescence) are often less important than standardized academic achievement data.

Implementation Steps Begin to build a system that integrates the cognitive-academic progress of students with their social and psychological growth:

1. Articulate a vision for educating the whole child as the primary focus of a school system's mission.

2. Explore areas of the curriculum in which age-specific issues and priorities need further attention and expansion.

3. Ensure that students' social-emotional needs are a priority in all classrooms, including individual needs, strengths, and developmental issues.

4. Make certain that every classroom is an inviting and engaging learning environment with a focus on the whole child.

5. Integrate into the instructional program key executive function skills and competencies, including goal setting, time management, and resource organization and management.

Pushback and Predictable Resistance Once again the traditional models of social and psychological services may work against a more holistic, integrated approach. Traditional silos may be challenged, provoking perceptions of boundary crossing or territorial encroachment.

BUILDING BLOCK 10: CAPITALIZING ON THE POWER OF PARENT, COMMUNITY, AND CROSS-INSTITUTIONAL PARTNERSHIPS

There are many regulatory barriers that will need to be removed to facilitate the growth of personalized learning. Seat-time requirements stand in the way of allowing students to get credit for online courses that could be taken outside of the school building. Personalized learning can take place year-round but the current school calendar in most cases still gives students a two-month summer vacation resulting in a significant setback to learning. This is particularly relevant to minority students and students in poverty who are most negatively affected by the time away from school.

Vision Increase the involvement and engagement of all stakeholders in the decision-making and problem-solving processes associated with transforming education as we know it.

Current Reality Most schools and districts are bound to traditional notions of governance and management. Top-down hierarchies associated with external and imposed mandates typically are the norm.

Implementation Steps

1. Begin exploring the possibilities of personalizing the governance structure: discuss what collaborative decision making might look like within the existing educational environment.

2. Examine ways in which decentralization of funding might be introduced, encouraging stakeholders within an educational setting to make decisions or give input about funding allocation.

3. Encourage all stakeholder groups to have a voice in school governance.

Pushback and Predictable Resistance Collaboration and partnership are more often the exception rather than the rule in most school environments.

Pushback can involve a range of phenomena, including fear of change, resistance to giving up power, and potential loss of control.

QUESTIONS FOR REFLECTION AND DISCUSSION BY STRATEGIC PLANNING TEAMS

1. To what extent do we agree with the principles and ideas of how to overcome these ten building blocks?

2. Where in our school or district do we see evidence of one or more of these building blocks being operational?

3. How would we sequence our approach to transforming these ten building blocks and personalizing our school or system?

4. What barriers and predictable resistance do we think we must face and deal with as we embark on this process?

Chapter 3

The Shifting Demographic Landscape

Personalizing Schools in Transition

When US Department of Education statistics projected that minorities would outnumber white students in public schools for the first time in fall 2014, headlines everywhere proclaimed a new "majority-minority" era (Figures 3.1 and 3.2). Even this oxymoronic term tells us a lot—suggesting that *majority* and *minority* aren't merely numerical indicators. Why would we still need to tag this new majority as a *minority*? If we're not talking about numbers, what defines *minority* within an educational context, and why might that distinction be important?

Some argue that these educational statistics—such as broader census demographics anticipating our inevitable transformation into a "majority-minority nation"—are based on inaccurate self-reporting. But such objections miss the point: the more relevant statistics show that these increasing minority populations are correlated with increasing school segregation, poverty, and compromised achievement—fewer resources, facilities, and advanced courses, coupled with higher dropout rates.

Increasing segregation in public schools doesn't just affect the achievement potential of minority students. As Gary Orfield (1983), the codirector of UCLA's Civil Rights Project, has forcefully argued, such trends finally "threaten the nation's success as a multiracial society." Here's the point: the latest demographic numbers don't need to be entirely accurate to recognize the dire need for significant change in our public schools.

The question then becomes how such shifting demographics should inform our substantial structural and policy changes in public education. Rather than continuing to scratch our heads as we "gosh and golly gee" like so many Gomer

Figure 3.1 Public Schools in the United States Projected to Be Majority-Minority in 2014

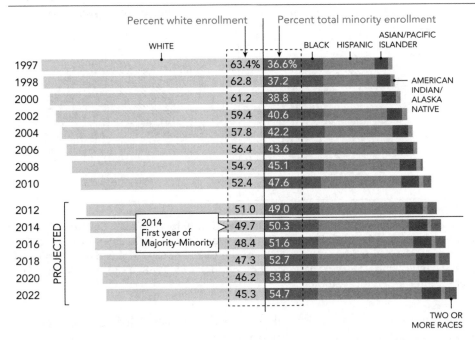

Note: Whites, blacks, Asian/Pacific Islander and American Indian/Alaska Native include only non-Hispanics. Hispanics are of any race. Prior to 2008, "two or more races" was not an available category. In 2008 and 2009, some students of both Asian origin and Hawaiian or Other Pacific Island origin were included in the two or more races category. In 2010 and 2011, all students of both Asian origin and Hawaiian or Other Pacific Islander origin were included in the two or more races category. In 2008, five states reported enrollment counts for students of two or more races. In 2009, 14 states reported enrollment counts for students of two or more races.

Actual and projected share of enrollment in public elementary and secondary schools, by race/ethnicity.
Source: Pew Research Center. Data from National Center for Education Statistics, US Department of Education.

Pyles, refusing to accept the reality of a world where whites are no longer the majority, how do we move our educational system ahead in a way that will be beneficial for all?

How many times will we prove philosopher Marshall McLuhan right: planning for the future by looking in our rearview mirrors? Why are we surprised to see Conestoga wagons, not Google cars? Perhaps we didn't listen closely enough when education analyst Diane Ravitch wrote about the troubled crusade or when others—over many decades—have called for radical reform.

Figure 3.2 Public School Enrollment

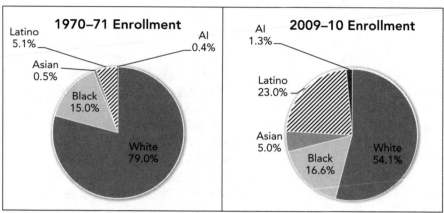

Note: AI = American Indian.

Source: U.S. Department of Education, National Center for Education Statistics, Common Core of Data (CCD), Public Elementary/Secondary School University Survey Data. Data prior to 1991 obtained from the analysis of the Office of Civil Rights data in Orfield, G. (1983). Public School Desegregation in the United States, 1968–1980. Washington, D.C.: Joint Center for Political Studies.

In the mid-1980s, an insightful yet presumptuously titled editorial appeared in the *Hartford Currant*: "The Forest Fire Theory of Economics as It Applies to Education; We Have Met the Enemy and It May Be Us, without Apologies to Pogo." Forest fires, the article argues, actually do some good—allowing new green trees and bushes to emerge from the wreckage of the old forest. Likewise, in economics, new businesses and approaches emerge from the ashes of a fiery recession. Perhaps education, the piece argued, needs its destructive yet revitalizing "forest fire."

Shifts in demographics alone do not tell the whole story nor compel most educators to throw the yellow penalty flag into the educational arena. But without question, the global education scene is experiencing seismic changes in *student needs*. In urban, suburban, and rural settings throughout this country, limited-English-proficient students are increasingly affecting schools and districts struggling to meet high-stakes accountability targets—and necessitating radically different approaches to curriculum, instruction, assessment, and student services.

There has never been a golden age of education. Let's dispense with any misleading nostalgia for a time that never was. Latinos and African Americans have long been underserved. It's not because our students of color are now a majority that education must be personalized; rather, it's because for too long we have not done well for some of our most needy students. We need a true moral awakening—and we need it now.

AN "AMERICAN PROBLEM": RECOGNIZING MINORITY NEEDS AS A FIRST STEP TOWARD PERSONALIZED EDUCATION

Some historical balance should be provided, because all is not bleak. When President Johnson signed the Civil Rights Act of 1964 into law, the baby boomer generation was in high school. At the time, the average teenager's mood was similar to what it had been for generations—a little self-centered, mostly oblivious to what was going on in the world, yet generally joyful, optimistic, and innocent. Little did they imagine the profound changes that would take place in their lifetimes.

The landmark legislation that President Lyndon Johnson signed into law on July 2, 1964, prohibited discrimination on the basis of race in public accommodations, in publicly owned or operated facilities, in employment and union membership, and in the registration of voters. Despite the many civil rights advances initiated by this legislation, President Lyndon Johnson recognized even then that it was just the beginning. "It's only the tail on the pig," he remarked to his speechwriter, Richard Goodwin (2014), "We ought to be going for the whole hog."

Johnson's quip resonates strongly today—perhaps especially for those baby boomers who have now gained the experience and perspective of grandparents; many struggle to maintain genuine optimism about the world in which their children and grandchildren will grow up—particularly in the face of the growing effects of income inequality paired with troubling trends toward resegregation in education.

This is not to suggest that nothing has been accomplished—but we don't want to be over Pollyannaish about the current state of education. To do so would be a disservice to those children who remain disenfranchised, to the significant achievement gaps that remain, and to the resegregation of schools that is undeniable in many parts of our country.

To mark the 50th anniversary of the Civil Rights Act, the US Census Bureau gathered key statistics measuring shifts in various achievements of different racial and ethnic groups between 1964 and 2012 (Table 3.1).

Sure, we can claim—and demonstrate—that much good has been accomplished in education over the past one hundred years. In fact, we should do this. At the

Table 3.1 Shifts in Achievement, by Race/Ethnicity

High School Graduates		
	1964	**2012**
Percentage of Blacks age 25 and over who completed at least four years of high school.	25.70	85.00
Number of Blacks 25 and over with at least four years of high school.	2.4 million	20.3 million
	1974	**2012**
Percentage of Hispanics age 25 and over who completed at least four years of high school.	36.50	65.00
Higher Education		
	1964	**2012**
Percentage of Blacks age 25 and over who completed at least four years of college.	3.90	21.20
Number of Blacks age 25 and over who had at least a bachelor's degree.	365,000	5.1 million
	1974	**2012**
Percentage of Hispanics age 25 and over who completed at least four years of college.	5.50	14.50

Source: U.S. Census Bureau, Current Population Survey, Annual Social and Economic Supplements. For information on confidentiality protection, sampling error, nonsampling error, and definitions, see www.census.gov/prod/techdoc/cps/cpsmar13.pdf.

same time that were patting ourselves on the back, however, we also have a responsibility to collectively say that we could and should be doing much more. There has not been a persistent, clarion call accepted by mainstream educators that we have failed too many students, left too much talent untapped, and are ultimately placing our country at risk.

Let's also be clear that we didn't get to this point in our education history without some real resistance, legal intervention, and legislative action. How many of us have brothers or sisters who went through schools without the support they needed? How should we feel about the reality that in 1976, the federal government had to step in to tell educators that education should be for all? And how many parent groups have been formed to advocate for students who were underserved or perhaps not served at all?

What can these challenges tell us about the best way to move education forward for all? Well, perhaps the first step is to acknowledge that we need to find a way to account for the various and varied concerns of this diverse population—to individualize and personalize our education system to address the needs of this ever-shifting population. To adapt a key point from Johnson's 1964 Civil Rights speech that seems as relevant today as ever, "There is no *minority* problem. There is no Southern problem or Northern problem. There is only an American problem."

THE ROLE OF PERSONALIZATION IN PREPARING STUDENTS FOR THE WORLD OF WORK

The "liberal arts" have taken a beating in recent years. There's hardly a politician remaining—left or right—who hasn't taken a cheap shot at the plunging value of a degree in anthropology, philosophy, or that ever-popular punching bag, English. Republicans such as Rick Scott or Mitt Romney have advocated for directly cutting funding for liberal arts disciplines, even slashing entire departments.

And despite being endlessly criticized by conservatives for his elitist, liberal-arts-loving snobbery, President Barack Obama himself took a swipe at art history during a 2014 speech in Wisconsin promoting job training and manufacturing careers: "A lot of young people no longer see the trades and skilled manufacturing as a viable career," Obama commented, before quickly assuring them, "I promise you, folks can make a lot more, potentially, with skilled manufacturing or the trades than they might with an art history degree."

Likewise, many of Obama's recent educational initiatives, including the Educate to Innovate program and his proposal for funding community colleges, are designed to create clear, coordinated pathways from high school technical training, community colleges, and internship opportunities usually to manufacturing, technology, and other STEM (Science, Technology, Engineering, and Mathematics) field jobs.

For educators, the question of what it means to truly prepare a student for the world of work in the 21st century—particularly in our current, perpetually tight job market—seems more complex than ever. Is the primary purpose of schooling, as the comments and policies of these politicians suggest, simply to narrowly prepare our students to perform specific technical skills for specific, predetermined positions?

This seems like a limiting and even potentially dangerous path to pursue. Don't we owe our children—and our communities, local and global—more than that? What about the idea that public education is intended to create literate, productive, participating citizens in order to sustain and enhance our democracy? How can we prepare our students not only for the world of work but also for a full, engaged life in the 21st century?

The skills needed to enter the working world today—particularly with the constant developments of technology—are vastly different than they were for previous generations. Similar to many in his generation, Mort Sherman's father never graduated from high school, working with his hands as a mechanic. Despite his limited education, his advice on this subject was deeply insightful: "You can choose to be a mechanic," he told me, "but don't let your bad choices make that decision for you." Are we preparing our children to make such an active choice?

Today, entering the workforce no longer means going out to the shops or the fields—getting your hands dirty. The skills, attitudes, and base knowledge needed to successfully navigate within the working world is very different. If vocational training will no longer even prepare our students to join the workforce in such a transitional economy, how can we fully equip them to be productive workers and engaged citizens?

Startling shifts in national and international economies are occurring throughout the world, especially the revolution resulting from technological innovation. Traditional notions of career pathways and career preparation are being challenged—and, in many cases, decimated in favor of a growing need for personalized career and technical education for a majority of students.

Faced with the daunting challenge of finding innovative, flexible approaches to personalizing public education while preparing students for this ever-changing working world, where can we look for models?—not abstract, theoretical examples but legitimate, realistic, road-tested methods and approaches to personalization that can be applied in a broader educational context. In the remainder of this chapter, we will look specifically at three key educational populations: special education, English language learner (ELL), and low socioeconomic status (SES) students. Each of these populations has specific needs; our current system has, with varying levels of success, devised personalized approaches to accommodate those needs. What can we learn from the successful programs and structures that have been developed, and how can we extend and enhance those successes further—and on a much broader scale?

IS THE BEST EDUCATION FOR THE HIGH ACHIEVER THE BEST EDUCATION FOR ALL? SPECIAL EDUCATION AS A MODEL FOR PERSONALIZATION

The goal of special education teachers is generally to create individualized education programs (IEPs) to meet the unique needs of their students. To be clear, there is a distinct difference between *individualizing* and *personalizing* educational programs, and it seems important to take a moment to clarify this distinction. A teacher working to create an individualized program is generally trying to assess the specific needs or challenges of the student, and develop methods or approaches that will enable that student to continue to follow the established curriculum being used in standard classes. So the ultimate goal of such IEPs is, through various tweaks, to enable the special ed student to access the same established curriculum being taught to mainstream students: to help the student adapt to the set curriculum rather than adapting the curriculum to the strengths and weaknesses of the student. The former is individualization; the latter is personalization.

But let's step back for a minute and consider what aspects of such individualization is working in current special education programming. Teaching special ed requires a tremendous amount of patience and empathy: teachers must be innovative and open-minded, often having to ignore the requirements in order to figure out ways to help their students. Certainly, we can learn something from special ed teachers who, day after day, approach their uniquely challenging jobs with flexibility and openness. Where would any one of these special ed students be without magnificent teachers who are constantly willing to adjust and adapt their approach to bring meaning and purpose to each task, each assignment, and each lesson?

But we can also learn something from special ed students. More often than not, these children, who are themselves facing overwhelming difficulties—physical, intellectual, and emotional—become not only our heroes but also our best teachers.

One student, for instance, who had transferred directly from war-torn Sierra Leone to a local Virginia high school, had the hatred, brutality, and viciousness of that war indelibly inscribed on her in the form of an amputated arm. Yet this cruel physical blow seemed to have only strengthened her spirit. The school's administrators, teachers, and staff were profoundly moved by her keen determination to make something of her life—to achieve goals she likely never would have even dreamt of in her home country. What drives students like this? How do they keep their chins up; their steps, however hindered, surging forward; and their unshakeable good humor intact—even helping others to keep going?

We all have similar stories of such astonishing students who make it against the odds. Many of us have been forever changed as we have watched a child with cancer struggle to live, a teenager fight against mental illness, a Down syndrome child spread joy, or a wheelchair-bound child who needs diapering and an aide, yet gives a smile to all around her. These children not only steal our hearts but also challenge all we know about motivation and living the good life.

The entire field of Special Education today is in major transition, reflecting the transformation imperative evident in all phases of modern education. The concept of the Individual Education Plan (IEP), for example, has undergone major revisions during the past decade. Most school systems today use what is called a "standards-based IEP," reinforcing the idea that all students must be successful in a rigorous core curriculum aligned with state and national expectations. Providing such an education requires clear expectations, but it also necessitates the educators understanding the learner, including his or her social, emotional, and relational needs. Truly effective specialized instruction—a necessity for every student today—requires clearly delineated learning goals, a range of learning options, and accommodations to ensure that how a student learns best is a fundamental part of his or her daily learning experience.

To *individualize* is a misnomer as it is currently applied in education. By tinkering with the mainstream curriculum, we have been trying to fit a square peg into a round hole. We shave off the edges, we rotate the peg, but it is never a really good fit. For a truly personalized approach, this is not the right mind-set: we need a new peg, not a slightly altered, ill-fitting version of the old one.

MAKING MULTILINGUALISM A RESOURCE, NOT A PROBLEM; ENGLISH LANGUAGE LEARNERS AS A MODEL FOR PERSONALIZATION

As suggested previously, the entire field of Special Education today is in major transition, reflecting the transformation imperative evident in all phases of modern education. The concept of the Individual Education Plan (IEP), for example, has undergone major revisions during the past decade. Most school systems today use what is called a 'standards-based IEP,' reinforcing the idea that all students must be successful in a rigorous core curriculum aligned with state and national expectations. Providing such an education requires clear expectations, but it also necessitates educators understanding the learner, including his or her social, emotional, and relational needs. Truly effective specialized instruction – a necessity for every student today – requires clearly delineated learning goals, a range of learning options, and accommodations to ensure that how a student learns best is a fundamental part of his or her daily learning experience.

As with special education students, ELL students—those for whom English is a second (or sometimes third or fourth) language—have much to teach us about the importance of personalization in education. A crucial shift has occurred in educational attitudes toward ELL students in our public schools. There was a time when the prevailing attitude was simply "learn English." Now, we have begun to recognize that there are often benefits to learning English as a second language. By considering a key example of best practices for addressing the needs of language minority students, especially those with limited English proficiency or lacking prior formalized school experience, we can take essential steps toward understanding how to personalize education more broadly.

The International High School (IHS) in Queens, New York, was founded in the mid-1980s as a collaborative project between the New York City Board of Education and LaGuardia Community College. With a diverse student population, culturally and economically, the school's focus is on providing alternative learning environments for students with limited English proficiency.

To address the varying linguistic needs of their student population, IHS has developed an instructional system wherein two instructors teach side by side: one teacher is focused on language-acquisition skills, and the other is primarily concerned with the subject or content under consideration. Such a dual teaching approach, integrating language learning within the natural context of the study of other academic subjects, has been hugely beneficial for ELL students—at IHS and at other high schools that have subsequently adopted this model for ELL instruction.

Notably, even as they focus on developing their students' English proficiency, these schools make it their mission to emphasize the inherent, independent value of a multilingual and multicultural educational experience. Fluency in languages other than English is treated as a resource—not just for the students but also for the class, school, and society.

The increasing evidence of second-language learners in schools today necessitates that students acquiring a language while learning the required content receive a truly personalized approach to education. Interestingly, this necessity reinforces many of the best practices associated with personalization. English Language Learners require a language rich learning environment in every classroom, with ongoing integrated focus upon reading, writing, speaking, and listening. Academically, vocabulary must be explicitly modeled and reinforced—with students encouraged to apply key words and phrases in a variety of modes and contexts.

As we consider how to personalize our educational model to account for the vast array of languages and cultures represented in our schools, especially in our inner city schools, we would be well served to incorporate strategies that are inclusive and inviting to ELL students—that respect and value what the learner has to offer.

WORLDS APART: LOW SOCIOECONOMIC STATUS STUDENTS AND THE NEED FOR PERSONALIZATION

Finally, it's important to think about what works—and what doesn't work—for students who face substantial socioeconomic disadvantages; this group includes not just students from homes where families are struggling to provide basic necessities but also students who are homeless or living in shelters. For such at-risk and severely economically challenged student populations, there is an absolute necessity for a comprehensive and holistic delivery of instructional, assessment, counseling, and related social services.

How do we find a way to implement these sorts of support systems for socioeconomically disadvantaged students? Compounding this challenge is the fact that severely socioeconomically depressed areas often closely border extremely affluent areas, exacerbating the disillusionment and eventual disengagement of many poor students. There are students in Virginia, for example, who have never even been to the National Mall in Washington, DC. Similar to so many other students across this country, they are trapped in a bubble of poverty.

National Public Radio's (2015) *This American Life* recently profiled an "exchange" program pioneered by two New York teachers a decade ago: the first, Lisa Greenbaum, teaches at University Heights High School, a public school located in the poorest district of the South Bronx, and the second, Angela Vassos, teaches at Fieldston, an eighteen-acre private school located on a hilltop only three miles away. University Heights is 97 percent African American and Hispanic; Fieldston is 70 percent white, with a tuition of $43,000 per year. The teachers hoped that introducing the two student populations would expand the experiences of both groups—give them insight into their own privileges or perceived limitations.

"Right now there is a popular idea in education—it pops up all over the place—about exposure; that exposure is particularly important for poor kids," observes Chana Joffe, the program's host, proceeding to explain: "You take a group of kids to tour a college campus, they'll be more likely to go to college. Or if you know someone who went to college, that'll help. The idea is that if you want a kid to move from one social class to another, that kid has to see what it looks like over there on the other side. Exposure is a tool for social change and economic mobility." After chronicling several University Heights students' reactions to this exchange, Joffe concludes that the other possible outcome of a glimpse at how the other half lives is that "it just sucks. You see how much you did not get, and it's shocking and painful."

This profile of two strikingly different schools in such close proximity not only perfectly illustrates the sort of poverty bubbles that are becoming increasingly common today but also highlights the many ways that students from a low SES background face challenges at every level of the education process. Even those low SES students who manage to make it to college—despite having less academic support and guidance and fewer academic opportunities (AP classes, extracurricular options, standardized test prep, etc.)—are far more likely to drop out during their first year (see Table 3.2).

In a traditional classroom in an economically disadvantaged area, the teacher alone can't possibly address all of these complex and interconnected issues. But

Table 3.2 Bachelor's Degree Percentage Completion Rates by First-Generation and Low-Income Status

	Attained Bachelor's Degree	Attained Associate's Degree or Other Credentials	Still Enrolled	Dropped Out
Low-income, first-generation	10.9	26.1	16.1	46.8
Low-income, not first-generation	24.1	18.8	16.5	40.6
First-generation, not low-income	24.9	21.8	15.5	37.9
Not low-income and not first-generation	54.0	9.3	13.4	23.3

Note: Low-income is defined as the student's family income falling at or below $25,000. First-generation is defined as students who come from families in which neither parent has earned a bachelor's degree or higher.

just as we've looked to special education teachers as potential models of the kind of empathy, patience, flexibility, and academic innovation that could be extended to a broader system of personalization, so might we consider how teachers in low SES schools have successfully employed similar qualities to meet the many challenges they face. We need to start talking about how we can draw on those approaches that are working in such economically strapped areas as we work toward changing the entire structure and approach to learning.

In education, too often change is focused on the classroom, and blame is focused on the teacher; instead, we would benefit by stepping back to see what we can learn from successful teachers and apply that to a whole school—or even a whole district.

AN IMPERATIVE FOR PERSONALIZATION: WE'RE MAD AS HELL, AND WE'RE NOT GOING TO TAKE THIS ANYMORE

What have we learned from thinking about how to effectively address the needs of these unique student populations? One thing is certain: we have a clear imperative. We need to do something radical—and soon. These experiences with special education, ELL, and low SES students teach us that we need to restructure schools, learning opportunities, and rethink the differences between individualized stopgaps and a genuinely personalized educational approach.

It's difficult to read one profile after another of variously disadvantaged students—kids with severe attention deficit problems, kids on the autism spectrum, kids with language barriers, kids who arrive in school without breakfast or basic measures of cleanliness and care—and face such an endless barrage of stories without becoming angry. Not so much angry for yourself but angry for these students—for the opportunities they will never get, for the skills and intelligence they *do* have that will never be acknowledged or valued, for the pure, unavoidable unfairness of the grinding poverty and growing inequality that seems to get more severe every day in our country.

It's tempting to imagine these students rising up, *Network* style, to declare their outrage and demand a revolution: "I'm mad as hell, and I'm not going to take this anymore!" What about if we, as adults, could start this revolution on their behalf?—throw open our windows and take a good, honest look at the state of public education in the United States. We need to recognize that there has been pushback among some segments of the population to current educational practices—a robust charter school movement. Finally, we don't really have a choice in this matter. It is our responsibility to take on personalization for *all* students in public education. A failure to do so may have catastrophic consequences, including the increasing polarization of our population, growing dangers of privatization and state takeover, and a growing lack of trust in education as a public institution.

QUESTIONS FOR REFLECTION AND DISCUSSION BY STRATEGIC PLANNING TEAMS

1. How are the demographics of our school system affecting our need for personalizing our approaches to data management, instructional ends, assessment, and learning?

2. What are our most immediate priorities in terms of the demographic priorities and shifts we are experiencing?

3. Which of the subgroups discussed in this chapter seem especially important? To what extent can we apply the suggestions and recommendations presented in this chapter to help them?

4. What should be our most immediate action steps?

5. What long-range action steps should we incorporate into our strategic planning process?

Chapter 4

The Road Less Traveled

Toward a Personalized Curriculum

THE RICH POSSIBILITIES OF A PERSONALIZED CURRICULUM

In schools throughout the United States—and the globally interconnected world today—personalization has become a hallmark of exemplary schools. At the new Discovery Elementary School in Arlington, Virginia, for example, the school's physical plant reinforces notions of curriculum as an immersive experience specifically targeted to the individual learner. According to the *Washington Post* (2015), each wing in this landmark school corresponds with a theme in the curriculum:

- Kindergartners start in the "backyard," with each classroom named for a backyard "critter" that students will learn about.

- With each grade, students broaden their horizons: second-graders, for example, are in the "ocean" and fifth-graders are in the "solar system" with classrooms named for astronomical features.

Flexibility is also essential for an effective personalized curriculum. At Innovations Early College High School in Salt Lake City, for example, students can begin their day as early as 7:00 a.m. and stay until 5:00 p.m. in the afternoon, with each student customizing his or her own schedule to take up to eight courses at a time. There are no periods—and no bells. Curriculum there becomes a proficiency-based process in which learners can finish any time they can demonstrate competency in applying required content standards.

Kenneth Grover, principal of Innovations Early College High School, surveyed students who were not doing well in school and discovered that they were bored because they either did not understand the material they were studying and the teacher moved on without them—or they knew the material and wanted to move on but were made to sit through one-size-fits-all lessons. As we will see throughout this book, he achieved his goal of creating a school that focused on the needs of the students—rather than the needs of adults.

The field of personalized curriculum is exploding today as parents, students, and key stakeholder groups push back against the tide of standardization and over-testing that is the sorry legacy of attempts to impose corporate quality-control models on an institution that is dealing with the complexity of educating complete human beings. Entrepreneurial firms such as NextLesson express a vision of "making learning relevant by engaging students in real-world problem solving through topics they care about …" (Dion Lim, CEO, personal communication). NextLesson makes use of what it calls "relevancy algorithms" and student interest discovery tools to help the curriculum become truly authentic and engaging for each learner.

PERSONALIZATION VERSUS STANDARDIZATION: THE GREAT CURRICULUM DICHOTOMY

We live in an era in which political ideologies are often in competition with notions about the purpose of education frequently dichotomized along ideological lines. Curriculum has become not only a hot topic these days but also a fractious and controversial one in many arenas. With the growing levels of student transience, socioeconomic differences, language diversity, and related issues described previously, we have to take a long and serious look at how exactly curriculum should function in a successful personalized school system.

Let's start with an operational definition. Generally, curriculum is considered to be a system's description of what students should know, do, and understand and a road map for when they should learn it—and how they should be taught it. Currently, however, the tide has turned toward a virtual obsession with discrete, standard-by-standard pacing guides mistakenly thought to ensure better test score performance.

Test preparation–oriented curriculum—a course of studies primarily focused on discrete concepts and skills tied to discrete state standards—has become a norm in many school districts, especially those in underperforming urban centers. We argue that a truly effective curriculum—particularly one that works for diverse student populations—must transcend traditional industrial and efficiency models of standardization and externalized pacing and embrace a holistic approach to educating the whole child.

Perhaps most important, we assert that curriculum as a system for promoting student learning is an idea powerfully confirmed by current educational and medical research. What exactly do we now know about how individuals learn best—and the ways we can promote the learning of every student? Consider five important research traditions that support the need for personalized curriculum:

1. **Learning as a holistic combination of body, heart, and mind.** We can go back to Plato on this one and move on to John Dewey and other great educational leaders, all of whom have suggested that learning rests in the learner. In effect, we do not teach others. We model and coach as guides on the side, but ultimately, all learning is an active process of making meaning on the part of the learner. True learning involves the interaction of mental and cognitive processes engaged by the affective and emotional reactions of the learner who must also be physically and actively involved in the learning process. All authentic learning is experiential and must place the learner at the center of his or her own learning process.

2. **Cognitive learning theory.** This educational research tradition reinforces that learning is a constructed act, a process in which the learner creates meaning through the power of experiential learning, inquiry, and problem-based investigation. Fundamentally, all genuine—and sustainable—learning is generated by the one who is learning, not received passively through lecture or didactic modeling. What educator Paulo Freire has called the "transmission" approach to education (in which the teacher dispenses or transmits information and the student passively receives it) is increasingly seen as inadequate and misinformed. Unless the student is at the heart of his or her own learning process, received knowledge becomes inert and nontransferable to new or unanticipated contexts, settings, and tasks.

3. **Neuroscience and executive function.**
   - Medical research—including the emerging field of educational theory based on insights from functional magnetic resonance imaging technology—confirms that learning is heavily brain-centered and involves activation of multiple brain systems.

- Personalized classrooms must reinforce students' capacity for use of executive function components such as activation of the working memory through engaged and purposeful learning tasks, reinforcement of self-regulation skills such as goal setting and time management, and support for metacognitive processes in which learners self-reflect on the extent to which they comprehend the purpose of what they are learning—and why they are learning it. Additionally, the negative effects of lower cognitive functions, including the flight-or-flight impulses generated by the amygdala, can be minimized when the student works in an engaging and supportive environment free of threat or anxiety.

4. **Creativity and self-expression as a biological necessity.** Mihaly Csikszent-mihalyi (1996) is the creator of the term *flow* as it applies to engaged learning. The author and researcher suggests that the most effective and sustainable learning occurs when the individual experiences challenges that are engaging and interesting but not so overwhelming as to activate fear and anxiety. Similarly, author Daniel Pink (2005) reminds us that the twenty-first-century workplace—including educational settings—should be sensitive to the ana-lytical and linear left hemisphere of the brain as well as the nonlinear and creative right hemisphere. In effect, both authors and others working today in the fields of creativity and creative problem solving suggest that it is a natural human impulse to be creative and self-expressive. Yet schools frequently encourage these impulses only in rare circumstances in favor of standardization and test-preparation protocols.

5. **A growing recognition that we express our intelligence differently and personally.** Perhaps the most significant principle underlying any model of personalized teaching and learning is the recognition that we all learn differently. Each of us constructs meaning in response to environments differently based on a host of filters and vantage points. Some of us prefer to learn visually, others through auditory channels, and others prefer tactual-kinesthetic interaction with their learning environment. Similarly, Howard Gardner (2011), Anthony Gregorc, Bernice McCarthy, and others suggest that we process information and make judgments in highly personalized ways. Some of us, for example, are concrete and sequential in our approach to learning new information or skills. Others are abstract and associational

or random in our approach. All of us react emotionally or affectively to different stimuli. Similarly, we differ in the ways in which we demonstrate intelligence. Some of us are linguistically adept whereas others excel in logical-mathematical processes. Some demonstrate physical prowess and experience the world by tangibly interacting with it. We all display varying degrees of visual and musical talent—just as we all take different approaches to the question of what it means to be human.

Schools and school districts considering the adoption of a philosophy of personalization will benefit from adopting a declaration of learning principles, reinforcing for stakeholder groups the importance and value of personalizing students' education. In the face of relentless demands for standardized test score improvements, it is critically essential for educational leaders to justify the need for personalization in the light of what we now know about the learning process.

CREATING A VISION FOR A PERSONALIZED 21ST CENTURY CURRICULUM

Based on what this expanding body of research tells us, what would an effective curriculum look like in a genuinely personalized school system? Although answers may vary, we assert that the following are non-negotiables if true personalization is to become a reality:

1. Curriculum must be seen as an **organic and integrated system** for facilitating, monitoring, and sustaining student learning.

2. All parts of that system must be **aligned** to achieve maximum learning outcomes, including the written, assessed, taught, supported, and learned curricula.

3. Learning outcomes articulated in the horizontal, vertical, and spiraling dimensions of a personalized curriculum system must include **not only cognitive-academic priorities but also social-relational, psychological, and physical learning.**

4. The process for **creating, monitoring, and sustaining** a personalized curriculum system must be a **collaborative** one that continually engages all key stakeholders in the process of determining what should be learned, when it should be learned, and how it should be learned.

5. The written curriculum needs to be **focused and realistic** in its scope but **ambitious** in the learning outcomes students are expected to master, including key domains of learning and 21st century workplace competencies.

6. The taught curriculum should be heavily **student-centered,** encouraging use of a variety of learning strategies and processes with the instructor as a genuine coach, guide, and mediator.

7. The assessed curriculum must take a **balanced approach** that minimizes the negative effects of test-driven accountability.

8. The supported curriculum should include **effective integration of technology** and related support resources and materials that enhance student engagement, imagination, and choice related to how they learn—and even what they learn.

9. When the learned curriculum extends from a personalized system such as this, **lifelong learning** becomes not only a philosophical priority but a true possibility.

CURRICULUM AS A PERSONALIZED SYSTEM OF LEARNING

A personalized curriculum is alive and constantly capable of changing and modifying itself to meet the needs of learners. Such a curriculum must be seen as an organic and integrated system for facilitating, monitoring, and sustaining student learning. To begin with, such a system must be vigilant in addressing the most significant student outcomes and avoid a tendency toward discrete standards taught in isolation.

For a curriculum system to become truly personalized, standards must be meaningful and reflective of 21st century priorities. In addition to what regional or state accreditation agencies may require, a personalized school system must offer a curriculum that reflects the best in curriculum designs. For example, what Jay McTighe and Grant Wiggins (2008) describe as Stage One, desired results must include not only core concepts and skills but also enduring understandings and essential questions. Desired results must reflect a commitment to a conceptually organized design arranged around key themes, unifying ideas, and universal concepts.

Similarly, curriculum designs must take into account student interests and learner profiles as well as emerging workplace and postsecondary competencies such as self-regulation, metacognition, collaboration in the work setting, creative problem solving, purposeful decision making, as well as a capacity for long-range strategic planning. Frequently, contemporary designs of curriculum emphasize required student academic-cognitive development at the expense of outcomes related to social-emotional and physical development as well.

Assessment—what McTighe and Wiggins call Stage Two evidence of student progress—must be balanced in a personalized system. It must move beyond traditional test-based models of progress monitoring to include a strong emphasis on diagnostic and formative assessments. Students must also be encouraged to take an active and sustained role in their own learning, clearly understanding evaluation criteria for which they are responsible, presented in the form of rubrics or related forms of scoring criteria. As suggested previously, whenever possible students should work directly with the teacher to determine personalized ways in which they can confirm their own progress and what they have learned. It is especially critical in a personalized curriculum system to ensure that standards-based assessment is open-ended enough to enable multiple modes of self-expression and self-evaluation.

Finally, the Stage Three learning plan as described by McTighe and Wiggins must take into account a gradual release of responsibility. As Robert J. Marzano (2011) in *The Art and Science of Teaching* has suggested, learning moves along a continuum. Although initial learning required more teacher involvement and modeling, eventually students must move toward growing levels of extension and refinement of their own learning until they can demonstrate independent transfer through authentic and meaningful performance tasks.

THE IMPORTANCE OF CURRICULUM ALIGNMENT IN A PERSONALIZED SCHOOL SYSTEM

A highly consistent component of schools that has proved effective in meeting the needs of diverse learners—especially students of poverty—is a powerfully aligned curriculum. According to Robert D. Barr and William H. Parrett in *The Kids Left*

Behind: Catching Up the Underachieving Children of Poverty (2007), a majority of research studies on highly effective schools cite a challenging and aligned curriculum to be a key to student success, especially for at-risk populations.

All parts of a curriculum system must be aligned to achieve maximum learning outcomes, including the written, assessed, taught, supported, and learned curricula. When a lack of alignment is present, stakeholders experience a sense of disconnect or dissonance, what Fenwick English (2007) and Allan Glatthorn (2000) refer to as a "hidden" curriculum. When a hidden curriculum is present, an imbalance is evident in one or more aspects of the curriculum as a system for guiding and informing learning. For example, an overemphasis on standardized, pick-the-right-answer testing can inadvertently lead to the absence of a balanced and authentic assessment process. Teachers in such situations frequently teach to the test, often leaving learners disengaged and mechanically compliant without real, transfer-based learning occurring.

A personalized system of curriculum is aligned in all its components. The vision and mission statements of the district—what English and Glatthorn call the "ideal" curriculum—should reflect a commitment to the importance and power of personalized learning. Similarly, the written curriculum should reflect a horizontal, vertical, and spiraling design that reinforces all students' proficiency as critical, creative, and self-regulated learners. As suggested previously, the design of the assessed curriculum should align and reinforce this commitment toward monitoring personalized and student-centered learning outcomes. Within the supported curriculum, all participants—including adults engaged in professional development—are a part of an integrated, holistic, and technology-enhanced system of lifelong learning. As a result, the learned curriculum clearly and consistently reflects the ideal, written, assessed, and taught curricula.

When clear alignment is absent, the unconscious aspects of the curriculum system become apparent. They are felt as inconsistencies, irregularities, and imbalances. Students and staff experience a sense that something is wrong, something is missing, or aspects of the curriculum are contradicting one another. In a personalized system of learning, the unconscious becomes conscious, transparent, and authentic.

EXPANDING THE FOCUS OUTCOMES TO ADDRESS THE WHOLE CHILD

All of the research cited previously—including the emerging body of research associated with improving the performance of diverse student populations—focused on the need to see the learner as a complete human being. Therefore, learning outcomes articulated in the horizontal, vertical, and spiraling dimensions of a personalized curriculum system must include not only cognitive-academic priorities but also social-relational, psychological, and physical learning.

A personalized educational system recognizes the unique nature of each learner. It also acknowledges that the whole learner is a combination of physical development needs, emotional developmental needs, and changing intellectual needs. Therefore, a personalized system recognizes that we progress differently and have differing perspectives, cultural traditions, and levels of developmental maturity.

Addressing the whole child requires that a curriculum system take into account the complexities of what it means to be human. Fundamentally, a great and personalized curriculum consistently works with the learner to answer the compelling why: *Why am I being asked to learn this? Why is this important to me? Why should I care about this?*

Additionally, a personalized system reinforces a taught curriculum that emphasizes a range of instructional and learning practices. Didactic, sage-on-the-stage behaviors are minimal. Experiential and inquiry-based learning that culminates in authentic projects and other forms of performance assessment are the norm. Independent, small-group, and large-group investigations and field experiences complement the modeling and shaping phases of the learning process.

Additionally, support services—including counseling, social, and psychological services—are accessible as complementary processes to enhance all students' learning, especially when intervening factors such as nutrition, psychological needs, or social-relational issues may interfere with the learning process.

ENGAGING ALL STAKEHOLDERS AS CURRICULUM DESIGNERS

Collaboration is key in the learning process. The capacity for small-group problem solving and decision making is a non-negotiable 21st century workplace competency cited recurrently by many employers and corporate heads. Therefore, the process for creating, monitoring, and sustaining a personalized curriculum system must be a collaborative one that continually engages all key stakeholders in the process of determining what should be learned, when it should be learned, and how it should be learned.

Stakeholders in this case should also include the students themselves who are engaged in the educational process. Periodic feedback-adjustment sessions should occur in classrooms and schools to determine what students consider to be working for them—and ways in which their workplace might be improved, enhanced, or extended. Similarly, parents and guardians should have access points to provide feedback and gain understanding about what their children are doing—and why they are doing it.

Great curriculum is organic and continually evolving. Teachers responsible for implementing it must take on a key role in helping to design and modify it. This process should include a range of program-evaluation processes that are teacher-centered and ongoing, including lesson study, action research, collaborative scoring of student work products and performances, and feedback loops involving administrators, central office, personnel, and instructors.

CREATING AN ASPIRATIONAL WRITTEN CURRICULUM

As suggested previously, the written curriculum needs to be focused and realistic in its scope but ambitious in the learning outcomes students are expected to master, including key domains of learning (e.g., critical thinking, creative expression, problem solving, decision making, investigation, and research) as well as what some have called 21st century workplace competencies (including strategic thinking, long-range planning, collaboration and share inquiry, conflict resolution, and empathy for alternative perspectives and approaches).

A key issue for consideration is the concept of purpose in educating students. This focus area is a recurrent concern for educators, politicians, and the public at large. Are we educating students to become ethical citizens, as Dewey suggested? Are we preparing them for the workplace? Are we committed to making learning an engaging part of students' lifelong maturation process? Or a combination of all three?

Ideally, a personalized learning system provides every student with an aspirational curriculum. That means that, first of all, students can see themselves in the curriculum content they are asked to study. They have a role in shaping and defining that content, including opportunities for them to explore independently topics and themes of interest to them but not a direct part of the required curriculum (e.g., a student gets to explore the music of the American Civil War while studying its history and impact).

Perhaps most important, an aspirational curriculum ensures that every student maximizes his or her success in academic settings and venues beyond the parameters of formal schooling. Students studying such a curriculum see and investigate their own potential, their own interests, and their own approaches to learning and working. Although emerging priorities such as a focus on career preparation in STEM (science, technology, engineering, and mathematics) are found everywhere in television and newspaper discussions of educational priorities, we need to reflect on what *Washington Post* columnist Fareed Zakaria (2015) describes as "our obsession with STEM education [making] it harder for Americans to innovate":

> Critical thinking is, in the end, the only way to protect American jobs.... In 2013, two Oxford scholars conducted a comprehensive study on employment and found that, for workers to avoid the computerization of their jobs, "they will have to acquire creative and social skills." ... The most valuable skills will be the ones that are uniquely human, that computers cannot quite figure out—yet. And for those jobs, and that life, you could not do better than to follow your passion, engage with a breadth of material in both science and the humanities, and perhaps above all, study the human condition.

SUSTAINING A STUDENT-CENTERED TAUGHT CURRICULUM

All of this leads to our assertion that the taught curriculum should be heavily student-centered, encouraging use of a variety of learning strategies and processes with the instructor being a genuine coach, guide, and mediator rather than dispenser of information. Ultimately, how students learn most effectively must guide and inform how they learn—and how they are taught.

We know a great deal now about the power of cooperative learning to engage and stimulate student learning, enhancing student abilities to creatively and critically deal with real-world scenarios, simulations, creative problem solving, and decision making. The taught curriculum needs to take advantage of such strategies. Similarly, it should ensure time for such processes by expediting students' acquisition of key declarative information (e.g., facts, concepts, generalizations, rules, theories, algorithms). The increasingly popular concept of the "flipped" curriculum reflects this commitment to an emphasis on personalization. Whenever possible, students should acquire information in what was traditionally presented in a lecture or textbook format via out-of-class access points such as electronic lectures and interactive technology-based information sessions.

The traditional notions of on-grade behavior will also come into question. Should we have grade-level designations—or are they artifacts of traditional industrialized and standardized notions of schooling? In a truly personalized environment, students will be able to progress at their own pace, supported by the coaching and monitoring of their teacher(s). Acceleration will be available to all when warranted. Similarly, students requiring extra support and intervention to master key concepts and skills will have the time and resources available to them for independent tutorials, coaching sessions, and related services.

TRANSFORMING THE ASSESSED CURRICULUM

A recurrent theme in this book is an emphasis on the need for more balanced and authentic measures of student progress. In effect, the assessed curriculum must take a balanced approach that minimizes the negative effects of test-driven accountability. A balanced approach to the assessed curriculum means true personalization related to acquiring and analyzing student progress-monitoring data.

In a personalized system, we should emphasize diagnostic assessments to discern and address students' varying readiness levels and needs for additional support in required concepts and skills development. Formative assessment should be the norm, providing a coaching-oriented environment in the classroom and school that engages learners and helps them become true self-evaluators and self-regulators in their learning process. Finally, we should see options for alternative forms of summative assessment tasks, encouraging student choice as to how they demonstrate proficiency and understanding in relationship to key learning outcomes.

The research is also very clear about standardized testing. Trends in Mathematics (TIMSS), National Assessment of Educational Progress (NAEP), and the Programme for International Student Assessment (PISA)—internationally recognized systems for comparative student progress monitoring—all confirm that the most successful state, regional, local, and national assessment models are associated with systems that emphasize a limited number of standards taught for depth of understanding. In high-performing educational systems such as in Singapore and Finland, curriculum is conceptually designed with a heavy emphasis on spiraling standards that students revisit with growing levels of understanding and independent transfer. In fact, the national curriculum of Finland is moving away from discrete subject matter and content distinctions in favor of integrated, problem- and project-based approaches to presenting and organizing curriculum content.

MAXIMIZING PERSONALIZATION THROUGH A TECHNOLOGY-DRIVEN SUPPORTED CURRICULUM

Technology—to present a true understatement—continues to transform our world and global marketplace. We are socially and technologically interconnected beings, and information is accessible twenty-four hours a day in real-time settings. Unfortunately, schools have frequently been unable to keep up with this transformation. Budget constraints and the rapid changes occurring in technology platforms sometimes work against true technology integration.

In spite of these issues, the supported curriculum in a personalized system should include effective integration of technology and related support resources and materials. The organic integration of technology can greatly enhance student engagement, imagination, and choice related to how they learn—and even what they learn.

At the same time, the supported curriculum must include frequent and ongoing opportunities for teachers and other instructional leaders to keep up with the latest advances in the field. Whiteboards and other technologies currently found in schools frequently do not take advantage of the potential for technology to individualize and personalize the learning process. The written curriculum should reflect a rich range of suggestions and options for students to learn independently, especially investigating avenues of personal interest and engagement.

Similarly, we need to do a much more extensive job of maximizing the use of technology to enhance student progress monitoring. In addition to data management and analysis, technology platforms can now provide us with multiple avenues for personalizing and individualizing student work products and objects of investigation. Contemporary technology can also help to personalize adult learning in the educational environment, including social networking and online learning.

LIFELONG LEARNING AS A CURRICULUM PRIORITY AND REALITY

When the learned curriculum extends from a personalized system such as described in this chapter, lifelong learning becomes a true possibility. In effect, everyone in a personalized school and district is a part of the learning and decision-making process. In such a system, curriculum is organic and alive, constantly evolving and transforming as differing student strengths and needs emerge—and are addressed successfully through a flexible system of curriculum implementation.

Finally, a commitment to personalizing the curriculum and all its various levels and components also requires a recognition that everyone affected by the system is a learning organism within that system. Feedback-adjustment loops must be integrated into the classroom, the school, and the district. A personalized education is a 21st century necessity. A curriculum system that emphasizes this principle and value is a critical part of ensuring that all learners succeed in this challenging, change-dominated, and technology-driven "flat" world.

QUESTIONS FOR REFLECTION AND DISCUSSION BY STRATEGIC PLANNING TEAMS

1. To what extent are the nine principles for a personalized curriculum system operational in our school or district?

2. In what areas of our curriculum are we showing a commitment to personalization?

3. In what areas do we need to place a greater focus on personalization?

4. Which areas of our curriculum system show the highest levels of alignment? Which areas show a lack of alignment?

5. To what extent—if any—do we have a hidden curriculum reflecting contradictions or misalignment in one or more areas of our curriculum system?

Chapter 5

Teaching and Learning in a Personalized School Environment

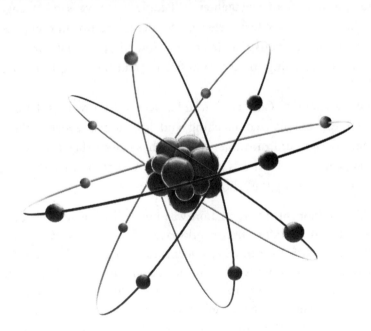

PORTRAITS OF PERSONALIZED TEACHING AND LEARNING

A rich tapestry emerges when portraits of personalized teaching and learning are combined. Its threads and design points all lead to relevance, authenticity, purpose, and student engagement. "People are always most engaged and effective when their work feels relevant. Students are no different," according to Thomas Layton (executive chairman of Upwork, personal communication). "They want their learning to have significance and meaning to their goals and dreams."

In a new Arlington County, Virginia, school—known as Discovery—the commitment to personalized teaching and learning is everywhere—from its flexible space design and movable walls, it physically defies traditional notions of industrial, centralized notions of education. According to a *Washington Post* (2015) article showcasing the school,

> [The] notion of differentiation was built into the school's design. The broad corridors have workspaces with clusters of stools and beanbag chairs to encourage students to work in small groups. Some classrooms have walls that can be drawn back if teachers want to co-teach a lesson. Each school day has a 30-minute period in the schedule when teachers can break their classes into small groups based on what they need—an extra math lesson, for example, or a reading coach—so that children get specialized attention.

Similarly, at Innovations Early College High School, the process of instruction has been radically shifted from traditional models and expectations. Rather than traditional dispensers of information or models of explicit instruction, teachers here are resources and mentors who have relinquished control of pacing and behavior management in favor of a much more progressive role: providing one-on-one coaching and small-group tutorials as a primary means of instructional delivery.

Every teacher at Innovations Early College High is assigned thirty students that they counsel and mentor throughout the four years of the program. The result is a caring and nurturing environment that is free of discipline and behavioral issues. The personalized pacing enables all students to be where they need to be and doing what they are motivated to be doing. Although still required to take state assessments, these students are allowed to take high-stakes tests three times a year to better align with their own pacing. The results of this instructional system are impressive, with radically increased graduation rates and college acceptance for students in a highly diverse population (i.e., 50 percent minority, 60 percent free and reduced meal recipients, 15 percent English learners, and 15 percent special education). To help make our recommendations for personalized instruction more concrete, you'll find a detailed description of this program later in the chapter.

A VISION FOR 21ST CENTURY INSTRUCTION

How would the teaching process change if learning environments were personalized rather than standardized? What we now know about the teaching-learning process confirms that great teaching is facilitative rather than didactic. A large number of longitudinal research studies (Trends in Science and Mathematics Studies, National Assessment of Educational Progress, Programme for International Student Assessment) all confirm that great teaching is mediated by the instructor, not presented through lecture. These studies suggest that students learn best when they are *not* forced to cover an excessive or unrealistic number of standards or respond to a curriculum that is mile-wide and inch-deep. Teaching in a personalized school environment, therefore, involves continuing professional learning (via lesson study and professional learning communities) to ensure that instructors employ research-based principles of learning, understand how to work with students to develop personalized learning plans, and make accommodations to maximize outcomes derived from those plans.

In a personalized school environment, teachers have options for maximizing student learning. They will not be confined to limited parameters extending from excessive test preparation or drill-and-kill activities related to high-stakes accountability measures. There will be clear and sustained evidence of one-on-one and small-group interactions rather than whole-group instruction. Lecture, for example, will be an exception—rather than the rule—of classrooms, eliminating traditional secondary models of classrooms as "mini-Harvards." The term "Mini-Harvard" originated in the 19th century when American education became more centralized, including the notion of academic disciplines and a liberal arts education. As Carnegie Units became the norm (identifying seat time for each content area), high schools in the United States were modeled upon Harvard University as a benchmark. Personalization will also involve allowance for student choice, including encouragement of learners to take the road less traveled.

We assert that there is also a close link between personalization and differentiation—but the two terms are not synonymous. *Personalization* is present when learners have direct and ongoing involvement in making choices about the curriculum content they wish to investigate, the learning processes they will use to acquire and integrate that content, and performance-based products they will generate to demonstrate the extent and parameters of their learning. By contrast, current models of *differentiation* tend to support the locus of control being in the teacher's hands—that is, the instructor determines how prescribed content will be differentiated to accommodate students' varying readiness levels, interests, and learner profiles.

In the personalized learning settings presented in this chapter, the locus of control is situated within the learners themselves. The teacher is a facilitator and partner in the decision-making process, establishing parameters for learning aligned with school or system curriculum standards and expectations. However, the personalization compact ensures that the teacher and student work together to identify a course (or courses) of action to maximize the learning process. For example, a fifth-grade unit on the American Revolution will, of necessity, address key facts, concepts, generalizations, and theories about major figures and events as well as the enduring legacy of the war. However, in a personalized environment, the student will also have options for exploring areas of interest that may not be a part of the traditional core curriculum. For example, a learner interested in music may be given options to learn about the music of the revolution, including classical, traditional, and folk music from the era and ways in which it reflects differing perspectives and viewpoints.

A vast range of options is available to teachers in a personalized environment. These can include—but are not limited to—learning centers, independent study projects, individualized learning packets, research scenarios, and opportunities for students to use multiple modalities when demonstrating the learning process. Similarly, extension activities and processes that are authentic and engaging include collaborative problem solving, scenarios and case studies, field experiences, internships, externships, and mentorship options. A personalized learning environment will also make use of a range of techniques and strategies frequently underused or overlooked in traditional or teacher-centric classrooms. The chapter will give descriptions, explanations, and real-life examples of such personalized learning processes.

A PROFILE OF A PERSONALIZED LEARNING SCHOOL: INNOVATIONS EARLY COLLEGE HIGH SCHOOL, SALT LAKE CITY, UTAH

Before we present specific case studies of personalized teaching and learning strategies in action, it may be useful to frame these ideas around an actual school known for its success in personalizing students' learning process. We've chosen as an exemplar the Innovations Early College High School in the Salt Lake City School District. The district describes the school as providing "a student-centered, personalized education" that focuses on learning through digital technology.

Following is a brief summary of the teaching-learning process in this innovative high school environment. Perhaps most importantly, students at Innovations Early College High School are a direct and important part of the decision-making process about what they learn and how they learn it. Through a comprehensive blended-learning approach, students can access learning opportunities any time during a twenty-four-hour period. Additionally, the district states that students can "utilize the power and scalability of technology to customize [their] education so that [they] may learn in their own style preference at their own pace."

A key feature of the school is its use of technology to remove traditional classroom constraints. Students can access learning any time and in any place, resulting in flexibility to take advantage of their peak learning time. As a result of this access to a technology-enhanced and personalized learning environment, students can spend as much time as they need to master curriculum content. The self-paced design of the curriculum enables high-achieving students to accelerate academically and enables struggling learners to spend as much time as they need to master the material they are learning.

In a school such as Innovations Early College High School, students have the chance to dynamically customize their schedule. This personalized approach greatly enhances their opportunities to explore topics, competencies, and themes of particular interest to them—including options related to enhancing their success in postsecondary educational settings and career pathways. Through their personalized educational plans, students may take anywhere from one to eight courses at a time, including completing courses as quickly as they demonstrate competency. The self-paced nature of their learning expands their access to new courses—rather than staying confined to the boundaries of traditional scheduling constraints.

What does the teaching-learning process look like at Innovations Early College High School? The Salt Lake City School District highlights the following technology-enhanced strategies available to students at the school:

- Comprehensive online and self-paced courses

- A rich multimedia learning environment that stresses interactivity among the learner, the instructor, and the content

- A curriculum that is competency-based and personalized to enable students to explore content in depth rather than breadth

- Assessment that is mastery-based, enabling on-the-spot monitoring of students' learning progression

- A modular approach to learning curriculum content, with the learning sequence organized around meaningful segments that spiral and build on one another

- Adaptive digital content, including options for students to make decisions about potential pathways for investigation and deeper inquiry

- Learning labs that enable personalized learning as well as student-student and student-teacher interactivity

- An emphasis on rigor and student engagement, including game-based and scenario-focused learning options as well as student-created digital content

- Embedded assessments that are organically (rather than mechanically) blended into the learning process, resulting in assessment becoming authentic and meaningful as a process for student self-regulation and self-adjustment

- Emphasis on social networking, including ongoing student collaboration and collective problem-solving and decision-making opportunities related to course content

Finally, Innovations Early College High School reinforces the assertion that a personalized education requires a rethinking of what constitutes the school environment itself. It models the power and value of cross-institutional partnerships. Partnered with the Salt Lake Community College and the Salt Lake District's Career and Technical Education Center shared campus, the school emphasizes the value of a seamless and visible transition between K–12 and higher education. The campus itself is open year-round with extended daily hours. It is equipped with labs, technology, and classrooms designed to emphasize collaborative as well as individualized learning. According to the school's website, the school is "a place where students are empowered and parents and teachers are liberated with real-time data about performance and progress … A place where every student has control over time, place, path, and pace."

PERSONALIZED APPROACHES TO LEARNING: CASE STUDIES IN ACTION

So, what teaching-learning behaviors and strategies should we see in any school or district that supports the concept of personalization? Any number of practices can address students' varying readiness levels, interests, and learner profiles. Here are a few top picks that we consider especially promising and noteworthy. We've included actual elementary, middle, and high school examples to make these practices even more tangible and accessible.

1. **Curriculum compacting.** Compacting enables the curriculum studied to expand or contract in terms of teacher-facilitated and independent-learning

options. It also encourages acceleration whenever possible, but ensures that tutorial, coaching, and remediation support is available when needed. The process of compacting requires a consistent approach to the monitoring of student progress, with a heavy emphasis on diagnostic preassessment as well as ongoing formative assessment feedback. In a third-grade reading class, for example, students engaged in a unit on folk literature (including fairy tales, legends, and myths) may all choose from a common body of literary selections. For students who demonstrate clear and immediate understanding of required texts, opportunities in a compacted curriculum should be available for them to extend and refine their learning through more independent reading selections, including more complex fiction derived from folk literature themes. Students who need extra coaching and support with reading comprehension and academic vocabulary, however, may benefit from more explicit and teacher-facilitated instruction focusing on key concepts such as theme, comparative text analysis, and fluency. Compacting is an essential element of personalization in all content areas.

2. **Tiered lessons and learning centers.** Tiered lessons and learning centers personalize core content to meet students' varying reading levels, background knowledge, interests, and learner profiles. Tiered lessons, for example, enable students to explore parallel content via differing reading selections (including tiered texts), tasks, processes, and modalities (e.g., written, oral presentation, performance, visual or performing arts, etc.). Tiered learning centers are designed to enable students with varying skill competencies to explore the same content with varied ways to demonstrate content mastery. Students in a fifth-grade unit on how a bill becomes law, for example, might study the legislative process through various reading selections (offering parallel content and text selections with varying Lexile or related reading levels). Tiered learning centers would enable either individual or shared involvement in a simulation or case study of a specific piece of legislation. Students would have various options for presenting their final projects, including written, multimedia, and oral presentations.

3. **Complex instruction.** A genuinely personalized learning environment reflects the best in what educational literature calls *complex instruction*. Teachers in such a setting use a variety of learning structures and processes to individualize learning activities and maximize student engagement and sense of authenticity and purpose. Didactic, lecture-oriented instruction

is minimal in a classroom reflecting complex instruction; when needed, blended learning via the flipped classroom enables students to access information in a lecture format through electronic means so that true coaching and investigation can occur when students and teacher are together. In a ninth-grade world history class, for example, students studying the European Renaissance will have multiple options for learning key concepts and skills. They may view Discovery Learning and other multimedia presentations on key historical and artistic figures from the era. In addition to core mandated reading selections, students will have options for independent reading selections about various aspects of humanism and its enduring influence. Students with a particular interest in the visual arts might study one or more significant painters or sculptors from the period. Those with an interest in architecture might create models of key buildings and technologies. Ideally, students will learn from one another at the conclusion of independent investigations, enhancing the range of what they know and how they communicate it.

4. **Learning contracts.** Contracts engage the student and teacher in a strategic planning process involving core content with agreed-on goals, deadlines, deliverables, and presentation options. The learning contract enables the student to express his or her personal interests in response to a particular content area. Contracts are ideal as a design template for project-based learning and culminating performance assessment tasks. They are also ideal for promoting students' use of executive function skills, including goal setting, time management, materials acquisition, metacognition, and pacing of the learning process. In a high school economics class, for example, students investigating the stock market can take various pathways to demonstrate their command of key concepts and skills, all of which can be spelled out in the teacher-student agreements articulated in the learning contract.

5. **Orbital studies.** While reinforcing students' exploration of the required core curriculum and required standards and competencies (i.e., the sun or center of the written curriculum), learning becomes personalized via student-generated extension projects (i.e., the planets orbiting the sun). Orbital studies as a concept is an ideal way for schools interested in personalization to remain consistent with the district's written curriculum while enhancing independent investigation and decision making on the

part of learners. In a middle school American history class unit on the US Civil War, for example, students may study together key issues such as the economic, political, and regional issues that gave rise to the war. They can then extend and refine their learning through an orbital studies project that provides deeper investigation of a topic or issue not directly covered by the class. A student interested in music, for example, might investigate the music of the North and South extending from this era, including how that music reflected the conflicting perspectives and viewpoints that gave rise to this ground-breaking event in US history.

6. **Independent study options.** A variation of orbital studies—independent study options—enable students to propose issues, topics, and processes that interest them (in relationship to required core curriculum content or content not typically addressed in that core) with a learning contract to guide and inform their independent investigation and product or performance generation. In a seventh-grade English class, for example, students learning about the elements of persuasive writing might extend and refine their learning through independent study options investigating persuasion through the centuries. One student, for example, might study advertising and marketing from an earlier historical era. Another might research how changing technologies have shaped and refined the nature of persuasive writing in the twenty-first century. Typically, an independent study option is a direct extension of the core content, whereas orbital studies allows for a greater degree of latitude and choice about the topic or focus area chosen by the student.

7. **Interest centers and interest groups.** These two interrelated processes involve providing structured learning center activities (aligned with unit or course content and related performance standards) that individuals or groups of students can investigate and complete. The centers, in turn, create opportunities for cooperative learning groups to investigate topics and issues of interest (related to either core unit content or extensions that enrich or extend it). Ideally, the interest centers themselves function as trigger points and catalysts for learners, enabling students to see a range of options to extend and refine their learning. Interest groups that form in response to the various interest centers can maximize their learning through cooperative learning structures, including forming JIGSAW expert groups. In turn, these

expert groups can teach other students about what their investigation has taught them. In an elementary unit on biomes, for example, various centers (including readings, photographs, maps, etc.) can be formed on different types of biomes found throughout the world. In addition to individuals or groups of students becoming experts on a specific biome by interacting with the center resources, they will have options for presenting their learning to others. Students might select a variety of presentation modalities, including a written report, multimedia presentation, dramatization, or video journal.

8. **Reflective journals and think logs.** Some personalization techniques can be relatively simple to implement but pay great dividends in student learning. Reflective journals and think logs are examples of efficient but highly productive tools for promoting student metacognition, that is, the capacity for self-monitoring and self-evaluation: *How well am I understanding this? To what extent are there parts of this I'm struggling with? How would I explain this to someone else?* Reflective journals can be used at key juncture points in any content area or grade level. Students maintain the journal as part of their academic notebook. At least once a day or period, learners are asked to stop, reflect, and consider the big ideas and important learnings they have achieved that day. Similarly, think logs ask students to stop and reflect periodically on their understanding and ease of use of a specific cognitive skill (e.g., analysis, synthesis, evaluation) or complex reasoning process (e.g., problem solving, decision making, creative expression). The reflective journal and think log reinforce students' use of habits of mind such as self-regulation, self-adjustment, self-reflection, and metacognition to develop conscious awareness and ownership of their own learning process.

9. **R.A.F.T. assignments.** Whenever a performance-based assessment task is given, students need clear directions and a clear understanding of purpose and performance requirements. However, such prompts can become more personalized in their approach if the instructor frames performance tasks around student-choice options. R.A.F.T. assignments enable students to take on different roles (R), address and modify products and performances for different audiences (A), choose from a range of formats for final products and performances (F), and pick from options for focus topics (T). An elementary unit on the geographic regions of Colonial America, for example, might culminate in students taking on the role of a regional

inhabitant from the era responsible for communicating about their living conditions and experiences. Their roles might include a choice of individuals representing varying social classes and economic strata as well as geographic locale. Their audience might include a family member in another country, a government official, or a reader of the student's choice. The format might include everything from a letter to an editorial to a series of daily journal entries. Finally, students can select from a range of topics, including descriptions of the harshness of their environment and living conditions to an analysis of the economic opportunities and challenges they confront as a part of the region they chose to write about.

10. **Culminating products and performances aligned with student learner profiles, including interests and areas of giftedness.** Whenever possible, personalized teaching-learning settings emphasize the importance of authenticity and performance-based approaches to summative assessment. Real-life and student-generated culminating products and performances enable student demonstrations of cumulative learning in realistic and purposeful ways, moving beyond traditional standardized tests. Ideally, such culminating projects also encourage students to reflect their own individual forms of giftedness, including the multiple ways that Howard Gardner reminds us students can display their intelligence (e.g., linguistic, logical-mathematics, spatial, musical, kinesthetic, naturalistic, philosophical, etc.). A high school American literature class, for example, might allow students at least once a grading period to explore content-related themes and texts of their own choosing. The culminating product or performance for each project can be determined by the student in partnership with the instructor. A unit on Fitzgerald's novel *The Great Gatsby,* for example, might have students investigate various aspects of the Jazz Age in the United States and Europe and choose various media or modes in which to express insights about a particular trend, cultural phenomenon, or historical issue.

11. **Cooperative learning structures.** Without question, the taught curriculum in a personalized learning environment capitalizes on the power of student interaction and collaboration. Once again, personalization suggests that learning is a personal act of constructing meaning in response to environmental stimuli. Cooperative learning structures place the learner at the

center of his or her own learning process. Simple structures such as listen-think-pair-share are immediate and on-the-spot ways for any instructor to encourage student sharing, testing of ideas, and reinforcement of meaning through one-on-one discourse. More complex cooperative learning structures such as the JIGSAW are built on the concept of the student as peer teacher, stressing options for students to become in-class experts on a topic or issue—and sharing their learning and conclusions with fellow peer investigators. Generally, we learn more about a topic, skill, or concept when we have to teach it to others.

SOME FINAL REFLECTIONS ON A PERSONALIZED TAUGHT CURRICULUM

We need to emphasize that the wide range of personalized teaching-learning strategies identified in these case studies represent a menu of options. True personalization, as we stress throughout this book, however, requires a comprehensive, holistic approach to schooling. It is insufficient to use personalized teaching strategies without establishing and sustaining a comprehensive infrastructure of personalization.

It is insufficient for the menu of options to be thought about and options selected periodically if those options do not occur within a unified approach to personalization. As the previous curriculum chapter reinforces (Chapter 4), the taught curriculum must coexist effectively and peacefully with the written, assessed, supported, and learned curricula. Simply using a personalization strategy here or there—whether frequently or sporadically—will not transform student learning and achievement if that use occurs void of a context of organizational personalization.

What does this mean for school districts exploring the concept of personalization? Here are some suggestions for beginning this dialogue:

- Make certain that your **ideal curriculum** (including your vision and mission statements and related public information materials) reinforce the value of personalization and its status as part of your organizational valuing system.

- Ensure that your **written curriculum** reflects best practices that encourage true personalized learning for all students, including many of the options articulated in the case studies section in this chapter.

- Provide **meaningful and sustained professional development** to support all instructors in becoming comfortable with personalization strategies, including understanding their value and significance in supporting and increasing student achievement.

- Integrate these personalized strategies for teaching and learning into **walk-through and related observation forms**, encouraging peer coaching and lesson study to ensure that instructors are operating with common ground and understanding about their use.

- Develop tools and processes for **assessing and monitoring** the extent to which classrooms in your school or district are making use of these strategies, including value-added studies discerning correlations between student achievement data and high levels of use of one or more of these strategies and practices.

- Build into your **feedback-adjustment loop** opportunities for staff and students to reflect on these personalization strategies—and their recommendations for modifying, enhancing, or expanding their use in all grades and content areas.

- Make certain that key **stakeholder groups**—including parents, guardians, boards of education, and community advocacy groups—are informed and in support of your commitment to personalization and the related teaching-learning strategies they should expect to observe when they visit classrooms.

QUESTIONS FOR REFLECTION AND DISCUSSION BY STRATEGIC PLANNING TEAMS

1. To what extent are the suggestions in this chapter feasible for implementation in our school or district?

2. As we discuss the profile of Innovations Early College High School, to what extent are its design elements applicable to our school or district?

3. Which of the personalized learning strategies and related case studies have particular relevance for use in our school or district?

4. What issues or barriers will we need to confront if we plan to implement the ideas and strategies recommended here? For example, what are the implications of this chapter for our strategic planning and professional development processes?

Chapter 6

Making Assessment Meaningful in 21st Century School Systems

PORTRAITS OF PERSONALIZED ASSESSMENT

As we've argued previously in this book, the perils of over-standardization are increasingly evident in schools today—especially in large urban centers. The overreliance on discrete standard-by-standard teaching and assessment (i.e., teaching to the test) reinforces an especially powerful need to transform assessment as we know it in public education. Valerie Truesdale (chief academic officer for Charlotte-Mecklenburg, North Carolina, schools) emphasizes, "In this large urban district, we are helping teachers get ready to make a true digital switch toward personalized learning. As you'll see on our website CMSLearns.org, we are combining new approaches to pacing, pathways, and play lists as well as habits of mind to place the learner at the center of our teaching-learning-assessment process."

Charlotte-Mecklenburg is adopting variations of a personalized medicine model to transform its approach to assessment. Through mobile technology enhancements and sustained professional development, teachers are using diagnostics to customize students' learning experience. The staff is at the heart of the assessment process, using action research to pose and investigate problems of practice that they can address and resolve as a collaborative team. According to Truesdale, the lines between and among the written, assessed, taught, and learned curricula are blurring in a collaborative commitment to promoting three major goals: student engagement, extended learning time, and student achievement for all learners.

A personalized assessment process truly puts the learner at the center of the learning process. Schools throughout the United States and world are beginning to use models for assessment that traditionally have been unique to the field of education. Personalized schools encourage teachers to become true diagnosticians, constantly observing, collecting, and analyzing data about their students' performance. Similar to any great clinician, personalized assessors in schools are in active communication with the learner—and collect and analyze data on not only students' cognitive and academic growth but also their social, emotional, relational, and physical growth and development.

Classrooms reflecting a personalized approach to assessment encourage student self-direction and self-monitoring. The learner is in partnership with the teacher to ensure comprehension, proficiency, and growing levels of independent application. Assessment in such classrooms and schools is embedded, forming a natural part of daily classroom interaction. All students understand clearly the learning targets for which they are responsible and engage actively with their teacher to ensure that they are progressing toward those targets successfully.

From elementary to university classrooms, personalized assessment also takes into account the power of discourse and interaction. Similar to successful workplaces today, team-based or small-group feedback and critiques—including peer and teacher coaching sessions—reinforce students' ability to activate and apply key executive function skills, including the following:

- Being clear about what they are to learn—and why they are expected to learn it

- Creating a road map or visual organizer that guides and informs student progress during a lesson or unit—not unlike a clear MapQuest for their learning journey

- Personal goal setting and strategic planning: *What am I expected to learn? What am I expected to do? What steps do I need to complete these tasks?*

- Comprehension monitoring (metacognition): *Am I understanding what I am learning? What questions do I need to have answered to clarify areas that are challenging me?*

WHERE HAVE WE COME FROM? WHERE ARE WE GOING?

The outworn industrial model of factory-like education has at its core the notion of standardization, not personalization. Value-added accountability at the heart of No Child Left Behind is essentially a corporate or business model that emphasizes discrete monitoring of aggregate and disaggregated performance on standardized tests. As we've suggested previously, the result has been a national obsession with test score results, diminishing or eliminating altogether a holistic education focused on the whole child's cognitive, academic, social-emotional, psychological, and physical growth and development.

As Gary Marx, author of *Twenty-One Trends for the 21ˢᵗ Century*, asserted:

> What we don't need is a scoreboard mentality that puts educational scores in the same league as football, baseball and soccer results.... Unfortunately, we sometimes narrow our focus to a few things that are easily tested and sure to make the front page. We become captives of the cognitive, and our goals become numbers or scores rather than fully educated people. We have our work cut out for us. Let's help our communities better understand the benefits and limitations of testing.... For the most part, we need to assess for clues, not solely for conclusions. Learning doesn't have a finish line. Education should always be a work in progress.

When we think about the astounding emphasis on standardized testing today—from its financial to its educational implications—we also need to see the consequences of over-testing. In a recent court case in Atlanta, for example, more than twenty teachers and administrators received extensive court cases for changing student answer sheets and giving cues to learners during test administration. The media are full of such cases that may, indeed, be extreme examples, but they serve as object lessons about our national obsession with testing.

What, then, will a personalized school district look like if its approach to assessment is not so rigidly standardized, test-driven, and fixated on misconceived notions of test preparation and related accountability? Although state and national standards do not appear to be going away any time soon, they will need to be balanced against a more comprehensive, rational, and personalized approach to student progress monitoring. Here are some recommended changes for your consideration:

1. Select **big-idea and conceptually challenging standards or learning goals** that are meaningful, complex, and worthy of being revisited over the course of a students' education.

2. Organize these learning outcomes around **conceptual bands or themes** that can provide meaningful organizing patterns, eliminating the current focus on discrete skills and concepts taught in isolation.

3. Ensure that these consensus-driven learning outcomes **reflect the full range of student development and the learning continuum,** including potential data points related to the cognitive, academic, social-emotional, psychological, and physical well-being of every student.

4. Develop a **comprehensive K–12 delineation** of what students are expected to learn, when they are expected to learn it, and how their progress will be monitored at key juncture points in their school career.

5. Make certain that all staff become **true data experts** capable of engaging in the range of diagnostic, formative, and summative assessment tasks and processes required to implement successfully a personalized approach to data collection, analysis, monitoring, and intervention.

6. Move beyond traditional notions of data collection sources (e.g., standardized convergent-response tests) in favor of **a balanced approach to data management,** including a focus on authentic culminating performance assessment tasks and projects.

7. Build a **data management platform** that enables educators to gain easy access to student diagnostic, formative, and summative assessment data, including access to student work products via electronic portfolios.

8. Ensure that **students take an active and ongoing role in their own data management** process, including reflections and action planning generated by the learner in partnership with the instructor: *How am I doing? To what extent do I understand what I am doing and why I am doing it? How effectively can I apply what I am learning to the world beyond the classroom? Where would I benefit from additional help or support?*

9. Explore the implications of a revised approach to **personalizing data management and assessment** in your school or district, including examining the possibility of a standards-based approach to reporting student progress: *For example, how might your progress report or report card need to change to reflect students' personal progress in the key domains you are monitoring?*

10. **Involve all stakeholders,** including parents and community members, in understanding and giving feedback on the emerging design of your

personalized assessment system: *Why is such a system important? What can I learn about my child's progress from this revised approach to data collection and evaluation?*

STARTING WITH MEANINGFUL, AUTHENTIC, AND LIFELONG LEARNING OUTCOMES

A personalized approach to assessment requires that school districts build consensus about what students should know, do, and understand throughout their school career. Specifically, districts need to achieve consensus about the following key question: *What is truly worth learning?* This question requires schools and districts to consider deeply the intellectual dispositions, habits of mind, work competencies, and intellectual knowledge that students will require as lifelong learners.

The delineation of meaningful outcomes also requires that personalized school systems consider goals related to students' development beyond their academic and intellectual growth. How, for example, will we monitor students' development of career competencies and access to emerging career pathways? How will every learner develop an awareness of and commitment to lifelong habits of healthy nutrition and physical well-being? What data will we use to monitor students' social and emotional development as they progress from elementary to middle to graduation and beyond?

Within the cognitive-academic domain, educators committed to personalization will need to use a kind of triage approach: *What exactly should go to make room for core intellectual skills and competencies?* As Robert J. Marzano (2011) points out in *What Works in Schools* and *The Art and Science of Teaching,* many school districts offer a mile-wide, inch-deep set of curriculum standards, resulting in a tendency of teachers to cover multiple outcomes superficially rather than teaching for depth of understanding. Similarly, William Schmidt (2005), director of the original TIMSS (Trends in Mathematics and Science Studies) report, says that the United States outpaces the rest of the world in the number of standards required for students to learn.

In a majority of high-performing countries identified in such international comparative studies as TIMSS and PISA (Programme for International Student Assessment), curriculum is limited in scope, providing time to encourage students' depth of understanding and transfer. Recently, countries such as Finland have eliminated discrete content areas and related academic standards in favor of project-based learning designed to monitor students' development of critical and analytical thinking, problem solving, and inquiry-based investigations.

A personalized written and assessed curriculum requires students to demonstrate a range of higher-order reasoning skills applied to the transfer and independent use of critical knowledge and skills. In a world history class, for example, learners explore themes and patterns of historical interaction taught through varying lenses and perspectives, including political, economic, and cultural historiography. In many high-performing countries, this focus on conceptual depth of understanding results in better standardized test performance because learners truly internalize and own the content, rather than mechanically retrieving it in discrete or isolated ways.

Additionally, personalized school systems will need to consider the inevitable requests, recommendations, and occasional outcries of employers within their community. The statistics are staggering and well publicized in the media today about adult illiteracy and the need for massive retraining as workers enter technical fields and corporate workplaces.

If an aspect of personalized learning is the preparation of students for success in a continually changing world of work, what exactly will schools need to teach, monitor, and reinforce in this area? Consider the following list of workplace-readiness skills for the Commonwealth of Virginia (identified by Virginia Employers and the Demographics and Workforce Group of the University of Virginia). How well do your students perform in the following areas? How much data do your schools have about student progress in the following domains?

Personal Qualities and People Skills

1. Positive work ethic
2. Integrity
3. Teamwork
4. Self-representation
5. Diversity awareness

6. Conflict resolution

7. Creativity and resourcefulness

Professional Knowledge and Skills

1. Speaking and listening

2. Reading and writing

3. Critical thinking and problem solving

4. Health and safety

5. Organizations, systems, and [organizational] climates

6. Lifelong learning

7. Job acquisition and advancement

8. Time, task, and resource management

9. Mathematics

10. Customer services

Technology Knowledge and Skills

1. Job-specific technologies

2. Information technology

3. Internet use and security

4. Telecommunications

To build a written curriculum that integrates the range of outcomes identified in this section is critical. An accompanying assessment system that truly monitors and provides appropriate coaching and intervention as required is also essential, but it will require a virtual change in paradigm if true personalization is to occur. Standardized testing must, of necessity, take on a much less powerful role, replaced by personalized and nuanced assessment tasks and processes that fully capture the range of what students are learning—and how they are developing as lifelong learners.

The movement toward personalization also reflects a growing demand within the business and governmental communities for graduates who demonstrate true 21st century workplace skills. Employers today require workers who are self-motivated, self-actualized, and exhibit a range of interpersonal and academic skills. These include such personal qualities and people skills as teamwork, collaboration, creativity, and resourcefulness. Workers in a 21st century environment require a range of communication skills as well as technology expertise.

THE NEED FOR BALANCED ASSESSMENT IN A PERSONALIZED SYSTEM

An essential component of an effective and personalized assessment system is the concept of a balanced approach. As we stress throughout this book, our national obsession with standardized testing has led to a variety of problems. The most significant of them is a clear emphasis on standardization and test-based accountability rather than assessment that truly promotes genuine student learning and understanding.

Although standardized testing is unlikely to go away any time soon, it is extremely useful to balance that priority against more authentic and genuine approaches to assessment. A test is essentially a form of summative evaluation, a determination of the extent to which a student has mastered certain standards at a certain degree of proficiency. Traditionally, however, selected-response tests are poor measures of the full range of what students truly know—or don't know. The repercussions of misguided test-preparation strategies are endemic to educational institutions today. The result is a great deal of measurement, without accompanying gains in student transfer, application, and lifelong learning. At best, a test measures a very limited amount of what a student really learns.

A balanced approach to assessment involves five major interrelated components:

1. **Diagnosis.** Ongoing collection, analysis, and use of meaningful diagnostic assessment data used to determine students' varying readiness levels, interests in the subject matter to be studied, and learner profiles.

2. **Formative assessment.** Using formal and informal data (gathered on-the-spot) to provide coaching and related feedback to individual learners, enabling them to self-monitor and adjust their learning as they progress to identified learning targets.

3. **Summative assessment.** Anchoring evaluation of student progress toward standards mastery around authentic, performance-based assessment tasks and projects, allowing student choice (whenever possible) about products and performances.

4. **Active staff collaboration in the data analysis process.** Ensuring that all staff members demonstrate a high degree of data literacy, including the ability to engage in lesson study, collaborative scoring of student work products and performances, and design and application of scoring rubrics and other criteria lists.

5. **Active student involvement in self-monitoring and self-regulation.** Encouraging students to take an active role in the assessment process, including collecting data about their own learning progress and engaging in self-reflection and self-evaluation reviews of their own work products as well as peer-response group activities.

ADDRESSING AN INHERENT ASSESSMENT PARADOX: TAKING A SYSTEMIC YET INDIVIDUALIZED APPROACH TO MONITORING STUDENT PROGRESS

In a personalized school system, the individual learner must be at the heart of the teaching-assessment-learning process. Paradoxically, however, an individualized approach to monitoring student progress cannot exist unless it occurs within a cohesive, data-literate system that encourages active monitoring and analysis of every student's progress. A personalized system, therefore, combines individual student profiles with aggregate and disaggregated portraits of the system as a whole.

Various types of individual student profiles can be used, from electronic portfolios to continually updated learner profiles captured in a systemic database. The challenge, however, is for systems to capture, analyze, and address the implications of a range of data domains. Clearly, most districts concern themselves with students' academic achievement, and, typically, standardized measures such as state accountability test performance. However, a fully personalized student profile must include other domains, including students' physical progress and health, indicators of social-emotional development, and career readiness.

Leaders of school systems moving toward personalization must recalibrate what data actually mean in their system—and what the purposes of analyzing really are. Systemic data profiles need to address universal (but often overlooked) questions such as the following:

1. How are our students growing and performing in relationship to **complex reasoning processes** such as critical and analytical reasoning, creative expression, problem solving, and decision making?

2. What **evidence** are we capturing that our students are progressing toward becoming active, engaged, and ethical citizens?

3. To what extent are our students making progress toward becoming proficient in **21st century workplace competencies** such as personal qualities, human relations skills, professional knowledge, and technology competence?

4. How are we ensuring that our students are **healthy** in physical and psychological ways, providing interventions and supports whenever necessary?

5. To what extent are we monitoring students' development of **executive function** skills such as use of working memory, goal setting, strategic planning, resource acquisition and use, and self-monitoring and metacognition?

CONCLUDING THOUGHTS ABOUT WHERE TO BEGIN

Today, public schools throughout the United States and our globally interconnected world are struggling with ways to overcome the negative effects of over-standardization, top-down-mandated accountability, and negative approaches to standardized test preparation. Here are some concluding thoughts about where to begin the process of personalizing your assessment process:

1. Make certain that your entire staff has a **shared philosophy** about the purpose(s) of assessment as a process for reinforcing student learning.

2. Provide **professional development** on the power of balanced assessment to effect change in student learning, including the clear need for diagnostic and formative assessment (including on-the-spot feedback for learners) to take precedence over summative assessment.

3. Plan backwards from **authentic, real-world performance assessment tasks.** How can we help all learners to demonstrate understanding and independent

transfer through authentic, meaningful, and engaging real-world scenarios, case studies, and problem-based investigations?

4. Help the **student become a key player in the assessment process,** including expanding the role of portfolio assessment, peer reviews and critiques, and peer coaching.

5. Make the assessment process **transparent.** Ensure that all stakeholders (including students and parents) understand what learners are expected to know, do, and understand and the connection of standards to authentic, real-world applications.

6. Move toward a model of **less is more.** Select power standards as a focus for your assessment process, determining which meta-skills and competencies are worthy of intensive performance assessment—and which concepts and skills can be assessed using lesser tools such as oral feedback or multiple-choice approaches.

QUESTIONS FOR REFLECTION AND DISCUSSION BY STRATEGIC PLANNING TEAMS

1. To what extent do we overemphasize standardized testing as a sole or primary data source for monitoring student achievement?

2. How effectively are we monitoring individual student progress against a variety of performance indicators?

3. Which elements of the personalized approach to assessment presented in this chapter seem especially promising or worthy of adoption?

4. What are some immediate and long-range action steps we might take to begin personalizing our assessment system?

Chapter 7

The Tech Revolution

Realizing Technology's True
Potential

Back in the mid-1970s the Commodore Pet made its debut in many classrooms. There are watches today that are more powerful than that desktop computer. All we could do with it was to write programs that would enable students to play simple games. For many years computer labs in schools were used to teach students to write programs. It wasn't until the mid-1980s that software began to appear that could drill students in simple mathematic and reading skills. By the late 1990s word processing began to revolutionize offices, replacing the typewriter. Toward the end of the twentieth century the Internet had come into its own and e-mail began to replace snail mail.

The first decade of the twenty-first century saw the transition from desktop to laptop to hand-held devices. Halfway through the second decade of the twenty-first-century wireless is the rage. No longer are we shackled to an electric outlet and a hard-wired Internet connection. We can surf the Web from just about anywhere.

We have also experienced significant advances in online courses and sophisticated software that have become powerful supplements to teaching and learning. With these resources a teacher can effectively diagnose where the student is on the instructional continuum.

However, at the beginning of this century educators and the public alike fell for a false promise of what technology could do to improve learning and close the achievement gap. Millions of dollars were spent by schools to buy computers and programs that would surely lead to higher achievement by all. That promise was not fully realized and critics began to doubt the impact that technology could have on education. Even the federal government pulled back on its funding for technology after not seeing the academic achievement gains that had been anticipated. We saw technology as the solution rather than the tool.

Nevertheless, technological advancements cannot be stopped. Smartphones and tablets are now devices that we cannot do without. We would sooner forget our wallet or pocketbook than our cell phone. Students have cell phones and many school districts around the country now allow all students to carry them. Using your own device is common practice within many school districts that cannot afford to provide each child with one.

Perhaps, some fear, the day might come when a sophisticated computer might be able to replace the teacher in the classroom. We tend to think not. However, that may have been the reason why the initial introduction of technology into our schools did not achieve the expected academic gains. We expected the tool to teach, but it cannot without the teacher.

Some of us recall that similar expectations came about with the television set. Back in the 1970s one of the authors was involved in a project in which two classrooms of students were exposed alternatively to a teacher and to a television set. The television played videos of lessons recorded by the teacher. In essence we would reduce the need for two teachers to one. The experiment was an abysmal failure. The television set was no replacement for a teacher.

Similarly the proliferation of programmed computers may have been seen as capable of producing greater learning while increasing class size and enabling the elimination of teaching positions. There were expectations that the substantial expenditures in technology would lead to greater cost efficiencies through the reduction in labor. However, the substantial expenditures did not result in either greater achievement or reductions in cost. Thus the federal government pulled back in technology investments in schools.

Don Soifer, executive vice president of the Lexington Institute, supports a true blended learning approach involving the combination of experiential learning opportunities enhanced through the power of technology-driven problem solving, decision making, and investigation. According to Soifer, however, antiquated models of governance, authority, and accountability

> make it hard to expand the reach of highly effective models to serve the number of students required to really move the needle on education growth and achievement in the ways we now know are possible. For this reason, the most exciting growth for blended and personalized learning models is going to be in traditional school districts around the country in the coming months and years.

REFLECTIONS ON THE ROLE OF TECHNOLOGY IN A PERSONALIZED SCHOOL AND SYSTEM

The potential for technology-enhanced personalization in schools today is enormous—and expanding exponentially as technologies expand, grow, and merge. According to William Hite (superintendent, Philadelphia Public School System), "Personalization is absolutely at the core of forming new schools. We are at a crucial juncture point: we have to re-imagine schools of the future. The world at large is much more interesting out of school than in school—we have to change that."

According to Hite and other superintendents interviewed for this book, technology can become a catalyst in helping educators develop conditions by which schools can thrive. "In a traditional hierarchical system, standardization chokes out any level of innovation." Hite stresses that we must involve individuals in rethinking their roles, implement necessary conditions, and promote flexibility in schedules and learning conditions. He cites the model of design-based learning, stressing that monitoring student progress must transcend standardized testing as a sole means of determining school and student achievement.

Hite and others suggest that a technology-driven process of teaching-assessment-learning should involve a competency-based toolkit approach. Technology enables a true developmental focus to guide education with every learner supported to enhance his or her own learning process—incorporating interests, needs, and aspirations. Although learning must be competency-based, the student should have the freedom to work independently as well as with teachers and peers to design personalized approaches to mastering those competencies.

Once again, we can see the vast potential of technology-enhanced personalization in the education students receive at Innovations Early College High School. During the course of a school day there, the learner can take advantage of a huge range of personalization options:

- Online, self-paced courses

- A rich range of multimedia-driven options for interactivity within the learning environment

- A deeper competency- and learner-centered approach to curriculum

- Mastery-focused skills and concept progression via technology-enhanced learning modules

- Access to online courses for college credit
- Adaptive digital content (accommodating varying readiness levels, student interests, and learner profiles)
- Learning labs using online tutorials and search engines
- Game-based learning options
- Student- and teacher-created content enhancements
- Delivery of instruction and access to resources via a digital course management system
- Embedded assessments (using different learning progressions and pacing)
- Social networks that promote student collaboration

WHAT IS THE FUTURE OF TECHNOLOGY AS A CATALYST FOR PERSONALIZATION IN SCHOOLS AND DISTRICTS?

Today we are finally beginning to recognize the rightful place of technology in the classroom. Technology is a powerful tool that in the hands of a well-trained teacher can result in significant achievement gains, enabling the realization of the holy grail of education, personalized learning.

We must, however, be careful not to make the same mistakes that were made a decade ago. Acquiring tools without properly training those who will be using them is a recipe for disaster. Alan November has been a pioneer in the field of instructional technology. He has trained probably thousands of teachers and administrators to use technology to expand learning well beyond what could be accomplished without it. A laptop in the hands of a student can be either a window to the world or simply an electronic version of a printed page that, other than saving paper and having the capacity to be updated, has no added value. Alan November has been a passionate advocate for the power of instructional technology in the hands of well-trained teachers.

We now have the capacity to supplement the printed word with pictures or videos that better expand on and explain the story or concept being taught. It is fairly common nowadays to be reading a newspaper article or a magazine online with embedded links that will take the reader to videos or additional content. We also have the capacity to establish an online community of learners who can help students collaborate with others and jointly solve problems and come up with creative solutions. Students can conduct research without leaving the classroom but can also receive instruction outside of the classroom.

Recently the Federal Communications Commission has significantly expanded the dollars available to school districts through the e-Rate program. The intent is to provide all schools with the necessary broadband capacity to provide expanded Internet connectivity to every classroom.

With school districts again spending billions of dollars on devices, software, and connectivity, educators must ensure that dollars are also available to train teachers to use the technology to improve instruction and attain greater student achievement. Broadband access and electronic devices alone will neither lead to greater achievement nor the closing of the achievement gap unless used by properly trained instructors. Our teachers must learn to become directors of learning rather than imparters of knowledge. They must become experts in diagnosing the needs of children. Technology will help them to do that.

Students will do work with programs that, with every keystroke, capture information on what the students know and do not know, how they problem solve, how they think. This digital profiling is currently available and intended to yield information that enables the selection of instructional material perfectly designed to meet the needs of the particular student and enhance uninterrupted progression. This is individual, learner-focused instruction rather than the traditional lesson plans designed for an entire class.

Currently blended learning models use the technology under the guidance and direction of a teacher. At the high school level there are credit recovery programs that enable a student to take an online course with teacher guidance and earn the necessary credits for graduation that would not have been earned in the traditional time line of a classroom structure. There are a growing number of virtual schools that provide home-based online instruction as an alternative to students attending a traditional school. The one-on-one laptop programs put these tools in the hands of each student, but that, by itself, is not personalized learning.

The technology currently exists to fully personalize learning, but there is more to it than just the technology. There are too many laws, rules, and regulations that stand in the way, including the graded, group-focused, K–12 organizational structure we have been saddled with for several centuries. We need a total transformation of how we currently organize for teaching and learning.

HOW CAN CURRENT AND FUTURE TECHNOLOGIES ADDRESS THE UNIQUE NEEDS AND TALENTS OF EVERY LEARNER?

The teaching process begins with assessing the needs of the students. The teacher uses that information to develop a lesson plan that will address those needs. Instructional materials are selected, the teacher teaches the lesson and may provide supplementary materials for the students to use. The traditional process focuses on a group of students, usually an entire class. In some cases some teachers may individualize and do it for subgroups of students in the class. Rarely is it done for each individual student unless it is a class of special needs students with formal IEPs required by law.

The personalized education we envision will in essence require the development of an IEP for each student in all classes, not just the special education program. We immediately recognize the difficulty of doing this when a teacher has twenty-five students in a class and is probably without a teaching assistant. But the technology is currently available that can make it possible.

Using a blended-model approach, for example, the teacher can identify a subgroup of students whose formative assessments have indicated that they are in a similar point in the instructional continuum. The teacher can bring that subgroup together, deliver a lesson, and then have them go on their laptops to engage in individual activities that would reinforce the lesson, assess the degree to which they have mastered the concept, and provide additional activities for those students who need the additional work until each student can demonstrate mastery before moving on to the next activity. Each student will proceed at his or her own pace until mastery is reached and the teacher will group and regroup students based on the degree of mastery attained.

This is obviously a very different process from the traditional class in which the teacher instructs the group as a whole and moves on regardless of whether all the students have mastered the lesson or not. The middle of the pack tends to be the focus of instruction, and perhaps a third of the class is bored because those students have already mastered the material and a third of the class is frustrated because those students are hopelessly lost.

In the future, profiling technology will be an invaluable resource in this process because the student profile goes beyond what the student knows and does not know and, based on previous responses, can fashion a program of instruction based on the student's likes and dislikes, what motivates the student, attention span, and extraneous knowledge and skills that can be introduced in the lesson plan to assist the student to better master the subject matter.

Students who are musically inclined might better learn if the material is embedded in music. Athletes might best learn from articles about their favorite sport. Poor readers can have audio accompany what is being read. English language learners can access audio and video to facilitate learning the meaning and pronunciation of the English word. All of this is currently available but it will be the teacher as director of learning who will coordinate and bring together the appropriate software program to meet the individual needs of each student.

HOW CAN EDUCATORS OVERCOME THE ROADBLOCKS AND HISTORICAL ISSUES ASSOCIATED WITH THE USE OF TECHNOLOGY?

Equity has always been an issue in the education of our students. It is often said that the best predictor of student achievement is the zip code. There is almost a perfect negative correlation between student achievement and poverty. The lower the poverty levels the higher the achievement and conversely the higher the poverty the lower the achievement. Schools with high concentrations of students eligible for free and reduced lunches do poorly whereas our highest achieving schools have a very low or no concentration of students eligible for free and reduced lunches.

Consequently, school systems that do not have the financial resources to provide their students and teachers with the technology necessary to personalize instruction will be forced to stick with the traditional group instruction–focused classroom. Rural systems that cannot access the Internet will have difficulty implementing a personalized education system.

Yet these are the students who are most in need of a personalized approach. These are the students who are being left behind by a system that requires them to learn at a pace that they are unable to maintain and are tested for mastery at a point when we know that they will fail and will forever be branded as failures.

The current system wants to raise standards for all but will do nothing to accommodate the needs of those children who we know will need more time and resources to reach mastery. For technology to do what it is capable of doing we must change to a performance-based accountability system in which the students are allowed the time that they need to reach mastery, not to specify that if mastery is not reached by all within the specified period of time those that do not make it are failures. We applaud senior citizens who earn a college degree in their sixties but any youngster who has not earned a high school diploma by the time he or she is eighteen is a failure. Performance should be the criterion for success, not time.

QUESTIONS FOR REFLECTION AND DISCUSSION BY STRATEGIC PLANNING TEAMS

1. What is the status of technology use and integration in our current district or school?

2. To what extent are we using technology to personalize the education of our students?

3. What gaps or impediments will we need to address in order to maximize technology's use as a catalyst for personalization?

4. What are our most immediate priorities in this area? What are our long-range priorities?

5. Where should we begin this part of our personalization journey?

Chapter 8

Transforming the System, Not Just the School

ESSENTIAL QUESTIONS

- What does it really mean to transform a school system through the process of personalization?
- In a personalized system, what will be the shifting roles of administrators, supervisors, and specialists?
- How can a personalized approach to social and psychological services support student achievement and well-being?
- What will be the role of parents and community members in a transformed and personalized system?
- How can cross-institutional partnerships enhance the effects of personalization?

So when all the variables discussed previously are in place, what exactly will a personalized school district look like? How will important roles such as administration, supervision, and student services transform themselves in the process? This final chapter will consider these questions as well as potentially dramatic changes in the roles and influence of parents, guardians, community members, and cross-institutional partnerships.

We contend that a personalized system is increasingly non-bureaucratic. Traditional industrial models of management and supervision—resting on top-down, hierarchical notions of control and conformity—will be replaced by true learning organizations. As organization development expert Peter Senge (1990) has asserted, true 21st century organizations demonstrate a continual process of self-awareness and a capacity for making appropriate and immediate changes when needed. All stakeholders are a part of decision-making and problem-solving processes. Additionally, all stakeholder groups in a personalized school system will share a common vision and sense of mission in their commitment to maximizing student achievement, minimizing unnecessary organizational distractors and impediments, and sustaining a belief and sense of intentionality about the importance of personalized lifelong learning.

Superintendents, principals, and other educational leaders interviewed for this publication show startling similarities in their views on what personalization might mean if fully integrating into a learning system and what its benefits are for diverse student populations today. Here are few reflections from key educational leaders today:

Kenneth Grover, principal, Innovations Early High School: "There is no failure at our school. No student gets an F. They continue with their coursework until they master 70 percent of the content and receive a P for passing. Higher achievement levels get letter grades. Although 30 percent of the students enter the school reading below grade level, all students graduate within a four-year period because the school operates year-round. The summer semester provides students the opportunity to move forward—not by taking remedial courses, but by being given the time and personalized services needed to achieve competency."

William Hite, superintendent, Philadelphia Public Schools: "Personalization is that which creates deep relationships so that students are well known to the adults in the school. Everything is more customized and more diversified to meet the array of backgrounds, readiness levels, interests, and needs of our students. Staff—especially the teaching staff—are first and foremost advisors to students. They are responsible for collaborative progress monitoring, self-reflection, being key points of contact for learners, and committed to a cyclical, spiraling approach to student development within the learning process. The design of the learning process is essential—and is the responsibility of all stakeholder groups—including students."

Valerie Truesdale, chief academic officer, Charlotte-Mecklenburg Public Schools: "Personalization involves a total revision of our thinking about school and school system infrastructures. In 2015–2016, for example, we will be expanding our personalized learning sites from fifteen to twenty-one schools. These schools are transforming their approaches to teaching, assessment, learning, administration, and counseling. Above all else, the learner is at the center of the learning process—not on the periphery. Personalization is a natural evolutionary progression from differentiation. Like personalized medicine, customized diagnostics must guide and inform decision making and problem solving. In the sites we have on board at this point, we have seen discipline referrals plummet dramatically with simultaneous jumps in reading and math results as benchmark starting points. For us, personalization has three key big ideas: student engagement, extended learning time, and powerful increases in student achievement results."

SHIFTING ROLES OF ADMINISTRATORS, SUPERVISORS, AND INSTRUCTIONAL SPECIALISTS

All of the current educational studies and leadership feedback on personalization reinforce a major paradigm shift in concepts of educational leadership. The superintendents, principals, teachers, and corporate heads leading this educational movement appear to be unanimous about the following:

1. **The necessity of consensus-driven performance targets achieved through a process of true personalization.** To start, we need once again to reinforce that the model for personalization that we are presenting here is not devoid of either standards or accountability targets. What this book attempts to support, however, is the necessity of transcending one-size-fits-all approaches to test preparation as a primary focus of contemporary schools. Personalized schools, districts, and regions must build consensus about (1) what all students are expected to know, do, and understand by key points in their education; (2) how every student will receive instruction, coaching, and support to achieve these consensus-driven performance targets; (3) techniques and processes for personalizing the assessment process to ensure that progress monitoring is sensitive and responsive to all students' varying readiness levels, interests, and learner profiles; (4) research-based instructional practices (including those reinforcing blended learning and digital and learner-centered approaches); and (5) strategies for promoting student ownership of and responsibility for the learning process.

2. **The need for decentralization.** Personalization inevitably requires that the school—not the central office—become the center of the learning and accountability process. A majority of resources must be situated within the school, including options for schools to personalize their selections of materials, instructional resources, and texts. Top-down mandates that fail to take into account the unique and diversified nature of the school population and staff inevitably reinforce a centralized accountability ethos that works against personalization. Just as teachers in personalized schools must use a clinical and diagnostic approach to identifying and addressing students' strengths and needs, central office staff must collaborate with school-based personnel and customize service delivery.

3. **The power of distributed leadership.** Another central tenet of personalization is the idea that leadership must be empowered at the closest levels of participation and responsibility. School-based staff—working in partnership with central office coach consultants—must have the freedom to determine how best to serve the needs of their students within the context of accountability parameters common to all sites within the district. Creating true communities of learning within each site should be a primary goal of personalization, including reinforcing staff use of an action research approach to problem solving and decision making. This process includes collaborative inquiry into individual and group-centered student achievement issues. It also requires that school-based staff be responsible for implementing centralized policies, regulations, and procedures in an effective but school-specific way. Teachers, counselors, and coaches must be empowered to become true instructional leaders rather than passive recipients of hierarchical mandates and dictates.

4. **The necessity of revisiting and refining roles of the central office.** Throughout the United States—and the world—today we are seeing a dramatic change in notions of centralized authority and leadership. Specifically, we are seeing individuals in roles such as supervisors, specialists, and curriculum developers become more like advisors and consultants to school-based staff rather than external evaluators and overseers of conformity. Central office personnel will become true teachers and professional learning experts, working closely with school-based staff to explore and implement the very best in personalized approaches to teaching, assessment, and learning. Similarly, when teachers need coaching, intervention, or extra support, central office personnel will deliver those services in a nurturing and caring way—one that is aligned in the best of what we know about the needs and expectations of the adult learner.

5. **The shifting nature of administration and supervision.** Administration and supervision in a personalized school and school system will come from collaborators and coaches more than externalized evaluators. Their primary mission must become facilitating the learning process of the adult learners with whom they work and for whom they are responsible as leaders. According to superintendent William Hite, the administrator or supervisor in

a personalized 21ˢᵗ century school will "facilitate and set conditions, support and monitor processes and strategies, ensure that time is used wisely and purposefully, demonstrate flexibility, open lines of communication among all stakeholders, and provide a customized and flexible set of structures to reinforce the learning process."

6. **The centrality of site-based and personalized professional learning.** As for the student in a personalized school or system, lifelong learning should be a priority for all professionals and support staff in that educational environment. Professional development must be customized and personalized to address the identified needs and interests of the individuals participating in it. Even more important, those individuals and groups should have an ongoing role in determining what professional learning is needed—and how best it will be provided. Blended learning for professional development is an inevitable necessity in this arena. The combination of direct and digital experiences, however, must be accompanied by extensive opportunities for participants to form true and intimate communities of learning. Once again, an action research approach is ideal, enabling participants to identify and explore an issue, topic, or decision—and work collaboratively to work together to research and resolve it.

PERSONALIZING SOCIAL AND PSYCHOLOGICAL SERVICES

In a personalized environment that addresses the needs of the whole child, social and psychological services will play an expanded and significant role. The role of counselor, for example, will inevitably shift toward greater levels of partnership with instructors as well as with the student as the primary client and service recipient. Students' social, emotional, and relational needs can be successfully incorporated into a personalized learning experience.

As suggested previously, current neuroscience and learning psychology teach us powerful lessons about the nature of human learning—and the ways in which schools sometimes contradict the way the human organism learns most effectively. In what is currently labeled *mindful* learning, students are actively engaged, challenged but not threatened by learning tasks, excited by creative alternatives and possibilities—and, whenever possible, physically engaged and experientially involved in authentic, real-world scenarios, case studies, simulations, and service learning.

Counselors, social workers, and psychologists can be invaluable partners in a personalized learning environment—working with instructors to help students feel emotionally safe and supported and socially engaged with peers. The new and emerging role of counselors and other positions in student service will inevitably require a more direct role of these human resources in an expanded classroom arena. Projects involving collaborative problem solving and decision making can provide powerful opportunities for students and instructors to examine the challenges and opportunities of active listening, collaboration skills, and related soft skills such as interpersonal communication, collaboration, empathy, and conflict resolution (often cited as necessities by employers hiring new staff).

Personalization for students with specific challenges—including students with limited English proficiency and disabilities—will necessitate flexible and on-the-spot access to counseling and related intervention services. These challenges will become increasingly apparent in an environment that stresses authenticity, rigor, and relevance through authentic performances and real-world products.

If the purpose of a 21st century personalized school or district is to prepare students for success in the challenging and continually changing global environment in which we live, students will need a holistic set of services accessible to them throughout their elementary, middle, and high school years. The siloed approach to student services we see in many districts currently will be replaced by a more organic and integrated design. Teachers in such a system will have the time to plan and monitor student progress with professionals on the social services side of the shop.

As a result, we should see increasingly authentic delivery of counseling and related services integrated into students' daily educational experience. Postsecondary education and career preparation and development, for example, will no longer be exceptions but will become integrated rules, a fundamental part of the written, supported, assessed, and taught curricula. All students will have individualized career and academic plans, beginning in the very earliest years. These plans will become a part of students' personal electronic portfolio with the learner in partnership with instructional and social service personnel to monitor learner progress and provide appropriate acceleration, enhancements, and interventions as needed.

Finally, our vision for a personalized school system also includes a commitment to twenty-four-hour accessibility to instructional, counseling, social, and psychological services as needed by the individual learner. Blended learning approaches—including electronic interaction technologies such as Skype—should ensure that if a student has a problem, he or she will have access to appropriate support systems whenever and wherever those services are needed.

TRANSFORMING THE ROLE OF PARENTS AND COMMUNITY MEMBERS

Parents as partners...community members sharing their expertise and interests...schools filled with the sounds of joyous children learning from their first teachers and influenced by the world around them...What educator hasn't held that vision in her head only to be brought back to reality when parents don't show up for back-to-school nights or fail to come to conferences designed to help shape a future for their children?

The challenge is enormous, made more difficult perhaps because parents and community members are not made to feel an integral part of the learning process from the first moment. So, no wonder when we want them to come to school, they don't feel connected to what we have created as one-off experiences.

The wonderful image of parents walking their children on the first day of school, kissing their dear ones goodbye, wiping a tear from their eyes, and then going off to work or home captures so well what we think should be changed through personalization of education. Coupled with this traditional image is the growing distance some parents and guardians feel from school because of social or cultural reasons.

Now imagine that those early days of learning don't start all the same day or the same time for all students. Rather, parents already have spent some time in school before the first day, a practice many schools have in place. And while in school, the families were helped to understand what the expectations would be, from behavior to academic standards. The time before school starts would be a time for learning to understand and support the environment of the school. Perhaps most important, parents would be given opportunities to experience how their children will be learning in a personalized environment. We need to create opportunities so that solving a math problem or taking on an entrepreneurial problem is accepted not as some crazy new fad but as the way children learn.

Personalized individual learning plans aren't sent home for parent signatures but involve the parents every step of the way, with signatures indicating the parents' understanding of the learning plan and accepting their role in supporting their children.

Many school districts have successfully created parent academies to support parents in learning languages or other literacies. We propose that every school have a parent academy that not only helps parents gain knowledge and skills necessary for their success but also improves the chances of success in their children's learning.

Open environments, personalized learning plans, and parent academies are all part of a holistic approach, which might be seen as fractals that give us a sense of connection. Just as we want to have a program for the whole child, so do we believe that a whole personalized environment is essential.

Within this school environment, within the community, and within the town or city's broader reach, community members are welcomed to the school. Of course we love it when dog owners bring in their pets to create a furry and welcoming space to spend time in, we love it when senior citizens volunteer in the classrooms, we so much appreciate the fire chief bringing a truck to school, and we are over the top with happiness when the mayor comes to read on Dr. Seuss Day. However, a personalized environment flexes those moments throughout the year to bring the community in and bring the children out in a seamless, natural way. However, a personalized environment flexes those moments throughout the year to bring the community in as well as allowing children to express themselves. This seamless approach to teaching and learning—emphasizing creative problem solving, scenarios, and authentic real-world experiences—greatly enhances students' sense of purpose, authenticity, engagement, and learning.

Here's the bottom line to parent and community involvement: Children need their parents and neighbors to succeed in a personalized environment. Because personalization creates unique pathways for children to get to the desired end point, we must view parents and community members as essential partners.

THE GROWING POWER OF CROSS-INSTITUTIONAL PARTNERSHIPS

The traditional organizational pattern of a school is very protective of its environment. Much of it has to do with the obligation that educators feel to the protection of the students they are responsible for. The *in-locus-parentis* concept is taken to heart, and all of us that have taught are aware of the great affection we develop for our students and the knowledge that we will protect them at all cost. Indeed, tragic events in schools ranging from mad gunmen intent on killing to the tornados that Mother Nature spins have yielded examples of teachers who have sacrificed their lives while protecting their students.

Most recently the fear of terrorist attacks and the acts of deranged individuals have turned school buildings into fortresses where all except students and staff must be kept out. This attitude often extends to other institutions and community organizations that are looking to provide support and services to the children within the school walls. Very often services and support that would be very beneficial to low-income and minority students are not taken advantage of and regarded as an intrusion to the school day. In educating the total child we have come to understand that there are extraneous factors that affect a child's ability to learn. Illness, hunger, poverty, and disruptive home environments are all issues that we know will affect a student's ability to learn and achieve.

There are many programs and institutions that are ready and willing to provide the services and support that will address many of these needs. Organizations such as Communities in Schools are designed to coordinate the services of community agencies within the school walls. United Way, Big Brothers Big Sisters, and the Boy and Girl Scouts of America are just a few of the many organizations that stand ready to come into the schools and help.

Unfortunately, these organizations are often incapable of scaling the wall of protection that schools have built up. The schools might graciously acknowledge the efforts of the community agencies but at the same time insist that their efforts be confined to the times when the children are not in school. Furthermore, the ability to share any information about the students that might be of help to the agency looking to provide the assistance and support cannot be made available because of privacy issues.

A personalized learning environment would greatly facilitate the delivery of needed support services to students. A personalized learning environment extends beyond the school walls well into the outside world. A personalized learning approach acknowledges and accepts that learning can take place anywhere and that the school building is just one site where this happens. The director of learning responsible for the child's learning plan can easily coordinate with the many institutions offering assistance and incorporates that service into the student's plan.

Such coordination can also extend beyond institutions that provide non-educational support services to organizations that provide workforce and career assistance as well as institutions of higher education. As students at the secondary level meet or are close to meeting the requirements for graduation, they can begin taking college credit–bearing courses at the institution's campus, online from home or at their school. Such arrangements are already in place in many high schools but a personalized environment would greatly facilitate the scheduling. Similarly, there would be many opportunities for youngsters to explore potential career choices by participating in apprenticeship programs with businesses, the process facilitated by the flexibility afforded by a personalized learning schedule.

The "maker" movement is a relatively new initiative that refers to the teaching of skill sets that enable students to make things. Three-D printers and laser cutters greatly facilitate the ability of most individuals to create things. In a way, this is the rebirth of the vocational education programs that lost popularity when they became the dumping ground for minority students who were not doing well academically. We abandoned vocational education and witnessed the evolution into more politically correct programs such as career and technical education, and now "maker" courses.

The reality is that we should always provide our students with career choices while we insist that all of our students meet the same standards that ensure that they are literate and capable of succeeding in a 21st century environment. A personalized learning approach is best suited to providing all students with the many pathways to a career, whether it be attendance at a four-year institution, a community college, or an accreditation program that will provide the skill set for gainful employment. Continual learning from cradle to grave will replace the K–16 pattern. That is the promise of a personalized learning approach.

SOME FINAL REMARKS AND OBSERVATIONS

A majority of the educators whose voices are heard in this book are in agreement about the necessity of transforming public education as we know it. From teachers and principals to superintendents and chief academic officers, there is a recognition that something major has to occur if education is to become a viable catalyst for preparing students for our dramatically changing world.

We hope that, for many readers, this book will be a starting point for this journey. For others, it may be a confirmation of what they already know or have experienced. The revitalization and transformation of an institution as traditional and sometimes hidebound as education is calling for a truly heroic commitment. Before concluding (in the next and final chapter) with our attempt to answer frequently posed questions about personalization, we'd like to acknowledge our partners in this journey with a few final remarks from our interview subjects:

William Hite, superintendent, Philadelphia Public Schools: "We are at a juncture point in public education—I consider the personalization of learning the greatest challenge of our time. Personalization is essential for a great and effective education for our diverse student populations. We must create deep relationships with our students—and our students with what they are studying. Our approach must become increasingly diverse and customized to meet the needs and strengths of the array of learners we are serving. This involves several non-negotiable elements, including a developmental (rather than fixed) focus on learning; design-based learning that addresses every student's interests, needs, and aspirations; learning goals that are meaningful, authentic, and competency-based; and instructional and assessment approaches that reinforce real-world problem solving and the imagination of the learner."

Kenneth Grover, principal, Innovations Early College High School: "One of the most impressive aspects of the school is how the teaching staff is utilized. Far from being the 'sage on the stage,' at Innovations teachers are resources and mentors who have relinquished control of pacing and behavior management to a much more progressive role—being a teacher by providing one-on-one and small-group instruction. Every teacher is assigned thirty students [whom] they counsel and mentor throughout the four years of the program. At graduation it is the mentor teacher who hands the student the high school diploma. This relationship has proven invaluable in the maintenance of a caring and nurturing environment that is free of discipline and behavior issues."

Valeria Truesdale, chief academic officer, Charlotte-Mecklenburg Public Schools: "We started [our road toward personalization] in 2012. At that time, none of our schools had the necessary infrastructure. We started by getting teachers ready for the digital switch ... personalized learning ... individual pacing ... and play lists of options and learning opportunities. . . . We reinforced everyone's habits of mind in terms of the dispositions necessary for personalizing education. . . . We are using Chrome Books for our middle schoolers. We are letting kids play an active role in their own education, having a say in what they are learning and how they are learning it. . . . The results in our schools using this approach have been powerful, with major growth in the areas of reading and mathematics."

Don Soifer, executive vice president, Lexington Institute: "Most of the most effective learning models we're seeing today were developed in charter schools or are based on models that were. Charters were designed to be laboratories for innovation and the success of high-performing blended learning charter schools has been an important development. But the charter governance model makes it difficult and slow to expand the reach of these highly effective models to serve the number of students required to really move the needle on education growth and achievement. For this reason, the most exciting growth for blended and personalized learning models is going to be in traditional school districts and schools in the coming months and years."

Dion Lim, founder and CEO of NextLesson: "Our vision is to make learning relevant by engaging students in real-world problem solving through topics they care about. . . . Educators have consistently told us that their top priorities are engaging students in developing critical thinking and making connections to the real world. [We are] building a comprehensive solution to map the world into the classroom with a personalized curriculum for students, easy standards-based lesson planning for teachers, and effective administration tools for school districts."

Before moving on to answering a few inevitable reader questions, we decided to end this book with a quote from T. S. Eliot in his poem "The Quartets":

> We shall not seek from exploration,
> And the end of all our exploring
> Will be to arrive, where we started,
> And know the place for the first time.

The movement toward personalizing modern education is a true hero's journey. We are all in this one together. Our sincere hope is that the ideas and recommendations we have presented here can be a starting point—or reinforcement—for your personal journey toward transforming the institution of education as we know it.

Epilogue: Answers to Ten Common Questions about Personalization

The vision we've presented in this book reflects a major trend in global education, that is, the recognition that our current approach to educating most students is woefully at odds with what they should truly be learning—and how they should be learning it. Inevitably, however, the call for a shift in the paradigm for education in general—and public education specifically—will trigger anxiety, skepticism, and questions. In this final section, we attempt to anticipate some of the inevitable questions and provide a starting point to help educators answer them when they are posed by individuals and stakeholder groups.

1. **How do you describe a personalized school system? How would you explain it succinctly so that a newcomer gets it?**

    A personalized school system places the individual learner at the center of the learning process. Every aspect of the system as a learning organization—from its written, assessed, supported, taught, and learned curricula to its budget design, leadership, and delivery of student services—is purposefully and intentionally focused on maximizing the achievement of every learner. A personalized system also focuses on the total individual—what has been referred to as the *whole child*. Everyone in that system is a lifelong learner committed to developing the physical, psychological, and social-emotional learning as well as well as the intellectual and academic success of everyone in that system. Adults as well as students are committed to their own learning process, as well as those around them.

2. **Why has personalization become such a popular theme these days?**

We believe that the recurrence of this theme in educational journals, news media, and emerging research studies underscores a collective recognition that our current approach to educating students is out-of-date and in radical need of transformation. The popularity of personalization as a universal motif and international discussion point emerges from a sense that our modern educational paradigm is on its last legs. We can all agree that standardization, test obsession, and misplaced accountability have led to some ineffective and even destructive practices. Compound that with the growing needs and unique perspectives of the younger generation, and you have a powerful cauldron bubbling over and demanding change. We simply do not design and deliver education for the twenty-first century: we remain stuck in the old industrial model that began at the turn of the twentieth century as industrialization and standardized efficiency became the controlling norm. We must deliver a personalized education to students living in the new millennium.

3. **How does the call for personalization reflect concerns about shifting demographics in many of school districts today, particularly those in urban settings?**

As we suggest throughout our book, the radically shifting demographics that characterize the United States and a majority of world civilizations today necessitate the need to customize and personalize educational delivery systems. The growing levels of second-language learners, transient and highly mobile families, and socioeconomic disparities common to virtually every region of the United States, especially its urban centers, suggest that a change in education must be forthcoming. Students who are hungry, emotionally unsettled, and disengaged truly cannot learn unless their complex physical, emotional, and social-relational needs are met as a part of the educational system in which they work and live. Personalization is an ideal, not a reality, for most students today. We assert, however, that the dramatic—even breathtaking—changes occurring in our student populations necessitate a new, transformative, and personalized way of educating every student today.

4. **What about funding a personalized school system? Won't it be enormously expensive to offer twenty-four-hour learning available to students anytime and anywhere?**

Educational funding is always an issue. Since 2008 and the Great Recession, we have seen countless urban centers struggling to make ends meet. The same is increasingly evident in urban and rural centers, as well. That said, however, we believe that personalization will not require radically more funding than the current industrial model of education we are supporting. It will, however, necessitate a radical rethinking of how educational monies are allocated. In a personalized system, for example, we will see a much greater emphasis on sustaining an organic, up-to-date technology infrastructure that supports blended learning available twenty-four hours a day for all students. Major expenditures will be necessary as curriculum is transformed, including a much greater outlay for lesson design, action research, and peer coaching as teachers assume a growing role and authority in educational design, decision making, and collaborative problem solving.

5. **Many of the schools you identify as exemplars of personalization seem to exist in a vacuum. For example, other schools in a district may not be delivering education in a personalized way. What are the implications of that?**

It is inevitable that in realizing the implementation of a new paradigm in any field—especially one as conservative and averse to change as education—there need to be pioneers and early adopters. Therefore, we believe that the personalization revolution must start with school sites that can be studied, replicated and used as benchmarks for others that follow. As a school within a district begins the process of personalization, it can be a nexus for research, investigation, and organizational study—with the institutionalized components proving to give the most value-added benefit being replicated in other sites. We recognize that the personalization process will not occur overnight. Inevitably, exemplar sites will need to be there first before the total system can fully transform itself.

6. **Where do you recommend that educators and stakeholder groups begin? This process seems overwhelming, at least on the face of it.**

Although within a system all parts reflect and affect the whole, certain subcomponents of a system can become priority nexus points in the process of personalizing education. In our opinion, the relationship between students and their teacher is the best and most universal starting point. As teachers work closely with their students to try out more personalized and differentiated approaches to the teaching and learning process, they can share their successes—and receive coaching and support from their peers—to perfect their use of such strategies. Inevitably, as a tipping point occurs and we see institutionalization of key strategies for personalization, the assessed curriculum will need to expand to account for these successes. The third priority extending from the first two will involve transforming the written curriculum. Increasingly, we should see less emphasis on more traditional forms of pacing guides and their typical one-size-fits-all approach in favor of a written curriculum that supports the individual progress of the learner. Curriculum guides, for example, will need to articulate desired outcomes but reinforce their achievement through a balanced approach to assessment and a clearly delineated learning plan for reinforcing personalization during a unit or course of study.

7. **What are the implications of personalization for other aspects of the educational arena? For example, how will schools of education need to change?**

That's probably another book in itself. Clearly, at national and international levels, there is a growing recognition that the preparation of teachers and administrators is a critically important issue. We believe that teacher and administrator certification programs and processes must become personalized. The individual professional needs direct, sustained, and experience-based learning opportunities to understand the realities of how students learn today, assessment practices designed to reinforce the learning process, and instructional practices that work for the twenty-first-century student. Theory and educational research embedded in preservice programs must be carefully integrated into real-world and authentic experiences that fully prepare the teacher or administrator to collaborate as partners in personalizing students' education. Similarly, we will see radical changes in requirements for entering the profession, with a growing respect and sense of professionalism evident as educators truly prepare students for the world today, not the world of one hundred years ago.

8. **What about boards of education? What are the implications of personalization for them?**

    Governance will shift dramatically in a personalized system. Mandates, dictums, policies, and regulations will need revision to reflect a system's commitment to personalizing students' education. Board members will become more collaborative partners in promoting the success of such a system rather than the politically fractious behaviors we often observe today, especially in highly politicized and underfunded urban centers. Boards—whether elected or appointed—will need to become educated about the purpose of education, the educational research justifying it, and ways to address concerns and questions that constituents may pose (especially those who favor more traditional and conservative models of education). Perhaps most important, boards must become advocates for this process, ensuring that budgets are approved and are sufficient to support the changes in the educational infrastructure needed to promote and sustain personalization.

9. **Aren't the challenges of personalization even more daunting for schools and districts in urban centers?**

    That is true if a specific urban center is highly fractious or politically divided. But you can argue that many school districts are like that today, regardless of their location or socioeconomic status. We believe that every school system can adopt many of the principles and practices we are advocating for in this book. Urban leaders—including boards of education—must work collaboratively to build consensus on the meaning of personalization, the role it will play in their individual districts and schools, and the extent to which allowances will be made for schools to vary in their approach to implementing personalization in their respective sites. Once again, we argue that the longest journey begins with the first steps: build consensus about philosophy, begin to identify personalization priorities, and determine inevitable resistance and obstacles—and plan appropriately to address them.

10. **How optimistic are you—really—that the vision you are presenting in this book can ever truly be realized?**

We remain somewhat cockeyed optimists. However, optimism is not necessarily naiveté. Each of the authors has experienced a growing groundswell of support for the concept of personalization as a controlling principle in education today. Educational leaders throughout the United States—and the world—seem to be in consensus that our students require more out of their education than we are currently giving them. We are thrilled that this publication can support that discourse—and we are optimistic that the abstractions we are presenting here will soon become realities in many schools and districts. The examples we cite in Chapter 3 are a testament to that eventuality. So, yes, we are indeed optimistic. It's nice to have that as one of the last words we write in this book.

References

Barr, Robert D. and William H. Parrett. (2007). *The Kids Left Behind: Catching Up the Underachieving Children of Poverty.* Bloomington, IN: Solution Tree.

Bloom, Benjamin Samuel (1976). *Human characteristics and school learning.* McGraw-Hill.

Burridge, Tom (2010-04-07). "Why Do Finland's Schools Get the Best Results?" BBC News. Retrieved 2012-06-27.

Csikszentmihalyil, Mihaly (1996). *Creativity: Flow and the Psychology of Discovery and Invention.* New York: Harper Perennial.

Educational Researcher (October 24, 2013). "A New Civil Rights Agenda for American Education," Tenth Annual Brown Lecture in Education Research. vol. 43, no. 6, p. 284.

English, Fenwick W. (September 2007). *The Art of Educational Leadership: Balancing Performance and Accountability.* Thousand Oaks, California: SAGE Publishing Company.

English, Fenwick W. & Steffy, Betty E. (September 2001). *Deep Curriculum Alignment: Creating a Level Playing Field for All Children on High Stakes Tests of Accountability.* Lanham, MD: Scarecrow Press.

Flesch, Rudolf (1986). *Why Johnny Can't Read: And What You Can Do About It.* William Morrow Paperbacks. Marx, Gary (November 2014). "Future-Focused Leadership," *AASA's School Administrator*, pp. 19–20.

Freire, Paulo (2007). *Pedagogy of the Oppressed.* New York: Continuum.

Gardner, Howard (2011). *Truth, beauty, and goodness reframed: Educating for the virtues in the 21st century.* New York: Basic Books.

Glatthorn, Allan (2000). *The Principal as Curriculum Leader: Shaping What Is Taught and Tested.* 2nd ed. Thousand Oaks, CA: Corwin Press.

Goodlad, John I. (2004). *A Place Called School*. McGraw-Hill Education.

Goodwin, Richard N. (December 19, 2014). "LBJ's speechwriter reflects on civil rights era and its lessons for race relations today". http://www.bostonglobe.com/opinion/2014/12/18

Illich, Ivan (2000). *Deschooling Society*. Marion Boyars Publishers Ltd.

National Public Radio (March 13, 2015). Episode 550: Three Miles. http://www.thisamericanlife.org/radio-archives/episode550/transcript

Orfield (1983). National Center for Education Statistics, U.S. Department of Education from *Public School Desegregation in the United States, 1968–1980*.

Pink, Daniel. (2005). *A Whole New Mind: Why Right-Brainers Will Rule the Future*. New York: Riverhead Books.

Robert J. Marzano (2011). *The Art and Science of Teaching*. Alexandria, VA: ASCD. Marx, Gary (November 2014)."Future-Focused Leadership," *AASA's School Administrator*, pp. 19–20.

Schmidt, William H., Wang, Sing Chi & McKnight Curtis (2005). "Curriculum Coherence: An Examination of U.S. Mathematics and Science Content Standards from an International Perspective" in *Journal of Curriculum Studies* vol. 37, no. 5, 525–559.

Senge, Peter (1990). *The Fifth Discipline: The art and practice of the learning organization*. New York: Doubleday.

Sizer, Ted R. (2004). *Horace's Compromise: The Dilemma of the American High School*. Boston: The Mariner Press.

Virginia Workplace Readiness Skills/Competencies. http://www.doe.virginia.gov/instruction/career_techinical/workplace_readiness/index.shtml Zakaria, Fareed (March 20, 2015). "*Why America's obsession with STEM education is dangerous.*" Outlook section of the Washington Post. P. B4.

Wiggins, Grant, and Jay McTighe. (2008). *Understanding by Design*. Alexandria, VA: ASCD.

Appendix: Accessing the Bonus Web Content

On our publisher's website you can access a number of tools accompanying *Personalizing 21st Century Education*. Just go to www.wiley.com/go/personalizing21, scroll down to the "Downloads" section, and you'll find the following supplementary materials:

- A facilitator's guide for anyone using the book in professional development. This guide contains training objectives, learning activities, tips for monitoring participant responses, and suggested follow-up activities.

- A PowerPoint slide deck recapping the book's main ideas and offering discussion questions and debate activities for each section.

- A sample syllabus for instructors using the book in an Educational Leadership course.

- A sample syllabus for instructors using the book in a Curriculum Design and Implementation course.

We hope you find these materials useful.

Index

McTighe, J., 57, 58
Mindful learning, 108
Mini-Harvards, 70
Minority, defining term, 36
Minority-majority era, 36
Monitoring, developing tools for, 80
Multilingualism, 45–46

N

National Assessment for Educational Progress
    (NAEP), 14–15, 64, 69
National Center for Education Statistics, 37
National Public Radio (NPR), 47
National Report Card, 14. *See also* National
    Assessment for Educational Progress (NAEP)
Network (movie), 49
Neuroscience, 54–55
New York City Board of Education, 45
NextLesson, 53, 115
No Child Left Behind, 83

O

Obama, B., 41
Observation forms, 80
Online learning, 28
Orbital studies, 75–76
Orfield, Gary, 36

P

Parents: capitalizing on power of, 32–33;
    transforming role of, 110–111
Parrett, William H., 58–59
Personal qualities and people skills, 87–88
Personalization: differentiation *versus,* 70;
    implications of, for boards of education, 123;
    implications of, for other aspects of educational
    arena, 122–123; individualizing *versus,* 43;
    popularity of, 120
Personalized curriculum: and addressing whole
    child, 60; and creating aspirational written
    curriculum, 61–62; creating vision for, 56–57;
    and curriculum as personalized system of
    learning, 57–58; and engaging all stakeholders
    as curriculum designers, 60; essential questions
    regarding, 52; and importance of curriculum
    alignment in personalized school system, 58–59;
    lifelong learning as priority and reality in, 65;
    and maximizing personalization through
    technology-driven supported curriculum,
    64–65; and personalization *versus*
    standardization, 53–56; and questions for
    reflection and discussion by strategic planning
    teams, 65–66; rich possibilities of, 52–53; and
    sustaining student-centered taught curriculum,
    62–63; and transforming assessed curriculum,
    63–64

Personalized data management/assessment, 85
Personalized education: creating vision for, 18–19;
    versus current system, 8–9; defining, 6–8;
    essential questions regarding, 2; and future of
    21st century education, 5; questions for
    reflection and discussion on, by strategic
    planning team, 11; vision for, in 21st century,
    9–11
Personalized educational system: building blocks
    for, 16–17; and capitalizing on power of parent,
    community, and cross-institutional partnerships
    (building block 10), 32–34; and creating vision
    for 21st century education (building block 1),
    18–19; and dealing with diversity (building
    block 2), 19–21; essential questions regarding,
    14; and identifying benchmarks and exemplars
    (building block 3), 21–22; and maximizing
    impact of technology and support resources
    (building block 7), 28–29; and personalized
    teaching and learning (building block 5), 24–26;
    and personalizing health, social, and
    psychological services (building block 9), 30–32;
    and personalizing leadership and governance,
    29–30; and transforming curriculum and
    programs of study (building block 4), 23–24;
    and transforming systems of accountability
    and making assessment meaningful (building
    block 6), 26–28
Personalized learning, 24–26; case studies in, 2–4,
    73–79; and curriculum as personalized system
    of learning, 57–58; essential questions
    regarding, 2; portraits of personalized teaching
    and, 68–69; and power of personalization, 4–5;
    and profile of personalized learning school
    (Innovations Early College High School), 71–73
Personalized school environment: essential
    questions regarding, 68; and personalized taught
    curriculum, 79–80; and portraits of
    personalized teaching and learning, 68–69;
    questions for reflection and discussion by
    strategic planning teams regarding, 80; and
    vision for personalized instruction, 69–71
Personalized teaching, 24–26; and learning, 68–69
Pew Research Center, 37
Philadelphia Public Schools, 105, 114
Pink, D., 55
PISA. *See* Programme for International Student
    Assessment
Plato, 54
Power, personalization of, 4–5
Professional knowledge and skills, 88
Programme for International Student Assessment
    (PISA), 64, 69, 86–87
Psychological services, personalizing, 30–32,
    108–110

Q

"Quartets" (Eliot), 116